MINDSWINGS

MINDSWINGS

The Thinking Way
to Better Golf

RICHARD MASTERS
AND
JOHN BURNS

AURUM PRESS

First published 1995 by Aurum Press Limited
25 Bedford Avenue, London WC1B 3AT

A catalogue record for this book is available from the British Library.

ISBN 1 85410 342 3

Typeset by Action Typesetting Limited, Gloucester

Printed and bound in Great Britain by
Hartnolls Ltd, Bodmin

CONTENTS

ONE

====

CAREFREE DRIVING

Painting is easy when you don't know how, but very difficult when you do

Edgar Degas

GOLF IS A GAME of the mind – the body is merely the medium through which we are obliged to play.

Although it is not possible to calculate or quantify the degree of skill involved in a golf shot, nor how much strength is required by a 200-yard drive, it is possible to evaluate the effect of the mind alone on the game of golf. And the scientifically unarguable conclusion is that the mind is exclusively and uniquely in absolute control of how we play our golf.

It does not matter if you are carrying twenty stones around the course, it does not matter if you have the odd finger missing, it does not matter whether you are young or old, short or tall, man or woman. What does matter is what is in your head; that alone determines how well you get the ball off the tee and into the hole.

When you come to think about it, it does not take an awful lot of strength or even skill to hit a golf ball a fair distance. All you need to do is use your head in the right way.

We would like you to forget everything you ever thought you had learned about how to play golf. Rid yourself of all those ghastly and ghosted instruction

1

books and magazine articles; remember only that when you pay to read how the top professionals recommend you should improve your game, you are subsidizing their next visit to their own gurus.

If you think physical strength has any real importance in golf, try exchanging your club for a length of garden hose with a lump of wood at the end. A smooth swing with the hosepipe, just as the pro may have told you to do with your driver, and you will never again attack the ball with brute force.

Whatever skill you bring to your golf is no more than a God-given ability, with the addition of just a little input provided by your pro when he first taught you how to stand, how to grip the club and how to swing it – the only fundamentals you require to play good golf.

There is no secret to playing golf. It requires no extra-ordinary abilities. It can be as uncomplicated and as painless as driving a car – once you have mastered the few fundamentals and practised a sequence of move-ments that will quickly become second nature to you.

Every car driver is confident (perhaps overly confi-dent) of his abilities on the road. Every golfer, from the youngest junior to the Masters champion, is unsure of (at least) some aspect of his game. And given enough time and sufficient rounds, every golfer will find some problem at some time with every part of his golf.

No driver would rush back to the driving school every time he scraped the kerb with a back wheel and expect the instructor to diagnose the cause of the misjudgment. In contrast, golfers tend to look for help and advice whenever any little part of their game goes out of line.

When we hit a golf ball we use what are called 'motor skills'. Motor skills are employed in every physical activity and, conveniently, there is a perfect parallel between their use when driving on the road and their use on the golf course. A motor skill – whether it relates to driving a car, using a typewriter, or hitting a golf ball –

2

is an action or sequence of actions that can be consciously learned, but which, once learned, is performed without the need for conscious thought.

This then is our compact. We are not going to seek to redefine the basics of the game – the feet, the legs, the arms, the shoulders, the grip. We are not going to show you an ideal swing or a perfect stance. But we are going to make you play better more of the time, in fact most of the time – and worse less of the time.

Walter Hagen, who hid nerves of steel beneath a debonair facade, used to say that if he hit six perfect shots that was as much as he could hope for in a good round. He won eleven majors – the US Open in 1914 and 1919, the US PGA Championship five times, first in 1921 and then four in a row from 1924, and four Open Championships (1922, 24, 28 and 29). Much of his greatness was due to his mastery of the recovery shot and his feel on the greens; in fact, Hagen was such a great player not because of his six 'perfect' shots in a round, but because of his ability to make the most of all the other sixty or so shots.

Golf – at every level – is a game of mis-hits. And judging by the similar-sounding expletives emanating from so many tees, legions of golfers appear to feel badly about them. The cheapest English dictionary and the costliest international coach both agree that a mis-hit is the result of a faulty stroke.

A game that is dominated by mis-hits and determined by low numbers demands that something has to give. So why not abandon the quest for that elusive perfect strike and concentrate on getting the mis-hits down the target line, and not into the rough or out of bounds? Of course this is not easy. But it can be done. And it is done by the more successful players. These are the golfers whose minds are not dominated by dreams of the textbook swing.

Jack Burke Jr, who won the Masters Tournament and the US PGA Championship (when it was match play) and was Player of the Year, all in 1956, described percentage golf as

> the science of playing the game with the shots of which you are capable but without the shots of which you are incapable. So it is a question of making up by guile, craft and common sense what you lack or never had. You can be beaten by people who play less well *better* than you play less well. It does not mean they are better players than you.

Whenever you see a hole-in-one on television the accompanying eulogy never suggests it might have been (and quite probably was) a bad shot. There is an unspoken assumption in golf that every movement that concludes with the ball dropping into the cup must be perfect, or, at the very least, very good. Yet Greg Norman says he can hit a perfect shot – and still be in a bunker.

When Lee Trevino aced the 17th of Pete Dye's desert holes in the 1987 Skins Game at PGA West he admitted he was lucky – not only to have won $175,000 with just that one shot, but also because it was luck that had put it straight in the hole. The usually wise-cracking Trevino could afford to be realistic (which is an often-used euphemism for 'honest' in matters of money and method) because, unusually among his sporting tribe, he has earned millions from golf without the benefit, or the cost, of coaching.

On every short hole in the world there are more perfectly hit shots that go through the back of the green than hit the pin or drop into the cup. Of more concern are the shots that are hooked, or sliced, or pushed. We are going to show you how you can keep those mis-hits down the target line. Better (by at least one, and maybe two shots) to have to chip back onto the green for two rather than to be hitting three off the tee.

The perfectly struck shot that goes wrong, just as

much as the badly hit ball that was always destined for disaster, is the product of a breakdown in the motor-skill department. Like most of life's embarrassments, the cause is usually that we have tried so very hard to do the right thing. And trying too hard to do the right thing is never the right thing to do.

There is no sport or game or pastime in the world where so many people resort to so many devices in order to improve their performance. Golfers buy more 'how to' instruction books each year than players of any other sport; and they also read more weekly and monthly magazines – largely for their instruction features. Every golfer who goes to his club pro for a lesson is contributing significantly to the multi-billion dollar industry which flourishes because of the misguided belief of millions of players that their golfing ability is dependent upon technology. This pilgrimage in search of perfection turns the gurus into millionaires and makes dupes out of the rest of us.

Like everybody else, we golfers are at once both the architects and the victims of our ambitions. By seeking to better ourselves we stand in great peril of making matters worse or, at best, after a brief and transitory improvement we lapse back into that *déjà vu* world where the old mistakes are compounded in direct proportion to our efforts to eradicate them. The more we strive to put into practice what we have learned through reading and coaching, the more mistakes we make. And the more mistakes we make, the harder we try to make it all come right – and the worse they become.

Perhaps it would be asking too much of the golf teacher to insist that he or she should always finish a lesson with an exhortation to 'practise what I've just taught you until it feels as if it is coming naturally . . . *and then forget it!*' All teachers, from nursery school to Oxbridge, want to leave a permanent impression upon their pupils. Even if unconsciously, there is a didactic overtone to the pro's advice to 'grip like this' or 'hold your elbow in here' or 'always extend through like so'. When he says goodbye until next week, and reminds you in the meantime to get out there and to practise what you've just been taught, he will have failed to show you what a world of difference there is between practising on the driving range and putting his teaching into practice out on the course. When you *practise* to *perfect* what you have been taught, you are reminding yourself how to perform the new or modified action. But when you go out on the course to put the rehearsed learning into *practice*, when you are addressing the ball and taking your swing, then you divest your mind totally of everything your pro said, everything you have learned. You must allow it to come to you naturally ... subconsciously.

Lest we should be misunderstood by a large section – though certainly not all – of the teaching tribe, we stress that we *do* think there are times – in some cases there are many times – when a golfer needs to have a lesson with his club pro, when the more advanced player needs help from a golf coach, or when a touring pro benefits from a session with his guru.

In conceding this we are more charitable than some observers. A recent entry in the apocrypha of the game – apocryphal only, we suspect, because its author prefers to remain anonymous, for obvious reasons – has it that a veteran caddie, while admitting during an Open Championship that he did not mind the modern players so much, added: 'It's the coaches that frighten me. I wouldn't let them wash my balls.'

No-one – unless they are one of a rare breed, such as a Trevino, a Nancy Lopez, or a Laura Davies – can start to play golf without acquiring some command of the fundamental principles with the help of a teaching professional. Nancy Lopez learned her fundamentals from her father Domingo on the municipal course at

Roswell, New Mexico. When she was eight he let her try her mother Marina's 4-wood. A year later she fitted into the peewee division of a tournament at Alamogordo, fifty miles southeast of the site of the first atomic bomb explosion in 1945. Because these eight- to twelve-year-olds were so small, they played only 27 holes – over three days. Nancy Lopez won by 110 strokes!

Her most sought-after present when she was a little nine-year-old was a Barbie doll, and Domingo gave her one for winning her first tournament. Three years later (when she was twelve) he came home with an armful of the dolls. She had just won the New Mexico Women's Amateur Championship. Domingo said: 'Nancy win – Nancy get every doll in the shop!'

When he taught her the basics of the game, Domingo told her: 'Come up real slow, come up real high, extend real far and hit the ball right in the sweet spot and keep hitting it until you hit it in the hole.' And even the first and only bit of advice she got from an expert did not affect her natural development. After his twelve-year-old daughter had won the state championship, Domingo asked Lee Trevino to look at her grip. 'For as long as it works,' Trevino said, 'don't touch it.' Most other pros would have changed her unconventional and unstylish swing long before she made the first of the many million dollars she was to win.

Nancy Lopez has a very upright stance. Unlike most touring professionals she keeps her left heel firmly planted on the ground as she makes her backswing. She turns her hips less than most top women golfers, but she turns her shoulders and coils the upper half of her body like a wound-up spring. Then she achieves tremendous power by pushing off on her right leg on the down-swing. Her follow-through is an extension of the swing, she could not stop it if she tried. The club wraps around her body and she is left fully facing the target.

'No, I never regret not going to a professional,' she

7

once told John Burns, before adding a typical under-statement,

> and I think I have my own individual swing. I don't think I
> could swing any differently. Daddy really taught me the
> basics and really made golf simple, and I think lots of times
> professionals confuse someone with weight-shifting and all
> the other things they think about. But Dad made it real
> simple and, you know, I was fortunate to have a lot of
> natural ability – so he didn't have to teach me. He just really
> talked to me about the game, just the basics and the concen-
> tration part of it. He had a positive attitude and that really
> helped me to develop my attitude about playing.

For those of us mere mortals who have been playing
for some time and who develop what to us may be
serious mechanical problems, there is little alternative
but to turn to a pro for help in diagnosing the trouble –
though we probably do not require a whole course of
lessons, which might lead to the unnecessary recon-
struction of our entire game.

Yogi Berra, former manager of the New York Mets,
used to say: 'Even a broken clock is right two times a
day.' Long before the cartoon character was named in
Berra's honour, another citizen of the Big Apple, an
expatriate Lancastrian, was bequeathing his golfing
aphorisms to posterity. Ernest Jones was an assistant pro
in Kent before he went to France in 1915 and lost his
right leg just below the knee. After the First World War
he went to America and became the professional at a
new women-only club at Glen View on Long Island. One
of the hundreds who flocked to him for advice was the
legendary Mildred 'Babe' Zaharias, who had set three
world athletics records at the Los Angeles Olympics in
1932 before turning to golf and winning the US Women's
Open three times. The Babe used to practise 'until there
was blood all over my hands and blood all over the
tape'. Then she went to see Ernest Jones, complaining
she had become 'fouled up in the mechanics of the

game'. Later, when the Glen View club itself became fouled up and the men took over, Jones moved indoors to downtown Manhattan where he continued to teach the game in a seventh-floor suite on Fifth Avenue.

Ernest Jones used to say:

> Those who try to teach golf as some kind of science try to take apart the arms and the shoulders and the hips and the legs and the head and the body. They want to turn every golfer into some kind of a worm that's been cut up into bits, with each part wriggling every which-way. That's how golfers develop what I call 'Paralysis by Analysis'.

Which is the same kind of paralysis you would suffer if when you drove your car you forced your brain to analyse every action, instead of using your natural skills. If you swung your clubs with the same relaxed confidence and competence with which you navigate the minefield of modern-day roads, your partners would never recognize your game and your handicap committee would not believe the cards you put in.

If you can separate the physical and the mental when you drive the car, you can do it almost as comfortably when you are on the golf course. In fact, when you are not on the course you are separating the two in most of the everyday things you do; but having started with the example of driving a motor car, let us stick with it for the moment. Then, if that is not sufficient, we will convince you that your motor skills, which you have never thought about before, are in fact your whole life force. Literally, they are your way of living.

When you first sat behind the wheel of a car you already knew that the steering wheel determined which way it was going to go, that the gear lever changed the engine speed (or something like that), that the foot pedal on the left had to be pressed by the left foot when you wanted to move the gear lever to another position, that the middle pedal was the brake to be operated by the right foot when that foot was not on the right-hand pedal (which was called the accelerator and did just that, it made the car go faster). So to slow down you were going to have to lift the right foot off the accelerator and transfer it onto the middle pedal and gently press. Then, as you were now learning, because you were slowing you would have to change gear. So your left foot would have to depress the left-hand pedal and at the same time you would take your left hand off the steering wheel and move the gear lever into another position. And so it went on. And so you were confused.

So you listened and you practised – without going anywhere. And then you had a first run, during which you stalled the engine as many times as later you would miss the ball when first you tried to drive that other projectile. Even when you had hesitantly (and miraculously) passed the driving test, for a long time your driving was, to say the least, somewhat jerky and erratic. The nearside wheels often ended up out of bounds on the kerb and always you had to think about how you were moving that gear lever.

You will never remember when, or why, or how it happened, but there was a moment long, long ago when you began to drive your car as if somehow the two of you had always belonged together, as if car and driver were one. You had given up consciously thinking about lifting your foot off one pedal and putting it on another, telling yourself when and how to change gear, remembering how to synchronize feet and hands. You had become an accomplished driver.

Long after you passed that test and officially had a licence to drive you entered into that hitherto unimagined state where the most natural thing in the world was to get into the car and let it all happen. For the first time you were able to think of other things, even able to take in what the voice on the car radio was saying. Driving your car had become second nature.

Perhaps you may be happier to think of the motor skills you use to drive your car as 'second nature'. Perhaps you are more comfortable doing things with your second nature than you are with your subconscious. If that is so, and it makes you feel more comfortable, use that second nature of yours and every time in future we refer to the subconscious tell yourself we mean to say 'second nature'. You will not have to think about telling yourself to do this because it will come to you through your second nature – subconsciously.

Perhaps you are already – subconsciously – drawing parallels between driving the car and driving a golf ball. But first consider some other examples in order to satisfy yourself that a motor skill is not only to do with driving motors.

A secretary does not consciously think about which finger should be placed on which typewriter key. She does not even look at her fingers as they strike the keyboard. When she learned to type she kept her eyes glued to her hands as she tapped each key, making a conscious effort to ensure she struck the right one each time. Subsequently it all became a natural, subconscious routine.

Do you think out every move when you fasten your tie? Every muscle movement when you pick up a glass or fork some food? Did you consciously decide which finger of which hand you would use to turn over the previous page? How come you are holding this book in whichever hand you are using? How did you decide which hand to use?

Ernest Jones used to recite a little poem to his Fifth Avenue golfing students:

> A centipede was happy quite
> Until a toad in fun
> Said 'Pray which leg goes after which?'

This put his mind in such a fix
He fell distracted in the ditch.

If you can walk down the street without telling yourself how to lift one foot and place it in front of the other, we promise that you have the potential to play better golf. We are not guaranteeing you will play better than your partners, but we are saying you will begin to make the best of your shots. Not just some of the time, but all of the time.

There is a fallacy, particularly prevalent in the world of golf, which has it that the influence of the mind in a sport is encapsulated in the principle of positive thinking. This is a dangerous idea. We want to use the mind in a much less constricted way than this. 'Think positively' is the clarion cry of those who pay only lip-service to the role of the mind in the game. Applied wisely and in context it can be an excellent dictum; appreciated as a beginning and not even a means to the end, it becomes a powerful ally.

Everything we do is the product of positive thought, otherwise we would not do it. You are now making a (subconsciously) positive decision to read these words. What the golfer needs to be taught is not so much to think positively as to stop thinking negatively.

Nick Faldo is not the most quoted or most quotable of the game's top players. But when in the summer of 1994 the man who had once been one of the world's best on the greens appeared to have reached a state of armed neutrality with his putter, he provided an eloquent explanation: 'I can leave them short from anywhere!'

If you so much as think that you can leave the ball short from anywhere, let alone underscoring your negative attitude by voicing such thoughts, then you will fulfil your self-prognosis. Faldo's is a classic example of negative thinking. By telling himself (and anyone who cared to listen to him) that his putting was awful, he was ensuring that he would continue to miss gettable shots.

When he realized that he was approaching the nadir of his putting prowess he should have been telling himself that he really was one of the world's best. That every putt was possible to make. That he could – and would – sink it. This way he would have created a confidence that is the acceptable face of positive thinking. Muhammad Ali used to tell us 'I am The Greatest' so often that finally he believed it himself . . . and then he was.

Even better than preventing yourself from thinking negatively is learning when not to think at all, or rather when not to articulate your thoughts, even to yourself. This is the state of being you need to practise when you are actually *playing* the game – which is not very often and not for very long.

For all its seductive attractiveness to player and follower, golf is the most anomalous of sports. It is the loneliest of pursuits, but it is always played with part-ners. With . . . but never against, because even in tournament golf the competition is between you and the course. And in match play the contest is more between you and yourself than between you and the course. It is some consolation that your partners are involved in similar contests, and at the end of the day the result is decided not by how you fared against them but how you fared comparatively, against either the course or your-self – or against both.

Golf takes longer to play than most other sports. Yet in a round of as much as four hours the golfer is in play only between two and three-and-a-half minutes. He gets to play the longer if he is still trying to break 100! With each stroke taking less than a couple of seconds the golfer spends very little time – not even two per cent of the game – in physical play. And that leaves one hell of a lot of time to be thinking about all the wrong things.

If the skill is all in the mind when you so simply and

smoothly change gear, it should come just as perfectly and painlessly and naturally when you move a golf club rather than a gear lever. We will forget the motoring analogy (consciously, at least) in a moment and consider only the golf swing. But before we do, let's be absolutely clear about motor skills.

Because any familiar set of physical actions – driving, typing, playing the piano, even eating dinner – requires considerable motor skill, this does not imply you do not have to think at all. You do not consciously think about the physical mechanics of changing gear, nor even consciously recognize that the engine is telling you it's time to do so. So it is that while your subconscious is controlling one action you can be thinking actively about other things . . . such as keeping within the speed limit, distancing yourself from other vehicles, obeying traffic signs and lights, and much else. And all the while the car is kept smoothly on the move.

When we say that you should dismiss all those swing-thoughts from your mind when you stand at the address and begin to take the club away, we do mean just that. This is not such an easy state of mind to achieve, but an excellent method of getting there is by using a pre-shot routine. Most professionals have their own highly individualistic rituals before striking every ball. And it is while you are going through your own pre-shot routine (which we shall discuss in detail in Chapter 4) that the clutter of rules which is worrying your mind about the next (or maybe still the last) shot will become submerged.

Now, before you stand up to the ball, when you are approaching the tee or walking forward along the fairway, when you are going through your pre-shot routine, right until the moment you address the ball – you should be thinking only necessary thoughts.

You must banish all negative thoughts. If the last hole was a disaster, it should have been forgotten, dismissed from your mind as if it had not happened. What went wrong on the 13th must not affect the 14th. If it was the best hole you have ever played – forget that, too. Don't ask yourself for a repeat performance. Don't try to make the 14th another perfect 13th. Just imagine it being a perfect 14th.

Even though you are only going to be actually playing the game for about a couple of minutes, in the three or four hours you are out on the course you are going to try to produce anything between 60 and 100 perfect swings. The temptation to talk yourself mentally through the swing is oppressive. And the only way to deal with any kind of temptation is to block it right out. This is not going to be easy. For lots of reasons.

When we strike the golf ball we are moving the club at such a speed that our brain cannot react fast enough to control it. When we take the club back the head describes an arc of about 32 feet; when the average handicap golfer swings downwards the head of the club will be travelling at about 100 miles an hour at impact and the ball will fly off at around 135mph. When someone like the longest-hitting US Tour professional John Daly attacks the ball he is probably swinging the clubhead at close to 150mph and sending the ball off at around 200mph.

Incidentally, when Daly tried his extended and unorthodox swing on the electronic shot analyser in the tented village at the 1992 Open at Muirfield, the diagnostic computer told his excitable fans that Daly's Killer Whale driver had punched the ball 380 yards. But, unable to contain itself, the machine concluded that the world's biggest hitter had 'too much weight on the back foot'! Photographic evidence shows that when he was at his prime Bobby Jones was on both toes at the moment of impact. Should we hit it that way? Was the first of the golf 'greats' wrong? Better that we do it our own way.

Once you have committed yourself to the downswing

the clubhead will strike the ball before you can even start to think about it. Messages take so long to register in the brain that when you feel the impact of the clubhead hitting the ball, the ball is already three feet away from you. One second after impact it will be 80 yards away from you.

To achieve this feat you will have utilized a whole range of moving parts – hands, wrists, arms, elbows, shoulders, upper body, thighs, knees, ankles, feet. And the driver in your hands is around $43^1/_2$ inches long with the face of the head $3^1/_2$ inches wide and probably 2 inches from top to bottom. It will have a loft anything from seven degrees up to thirteen. If you're an average player with a typical 8.5-degree driver then you are endeavouring to launch a 1.68-inch ball weighing no more than 1.62 ounces at an initial velocity of 250 feet (or 72.6 metres) per second using a club which has only four degrees more loft than your putter!

Attempting to launch a one-and-a-half inch ball standing side-on with the hands $43^1/_2$ inches away and also at the side of the ball does not allow much room for error. Half an inch to the left with the face of the club at the strike position and the ball will be out of bounds on the left; the same to the right and it will be out on the right; the same half-inch in the air and you will have topped the ball; and half an inch too low and the result will be a deep divot.

Perhaps you went to the pro during the week and he found a fault in your grip (or whatever). Now, for the first time since your lesson, you are standing up to the ball on the first tee all primed and ready with the remedy. 'Think positive' is the maxim, isn't it? So you think you have beaten it . . . this is what the pro said to do. You keep his advice at the front of your mind as you address the ball – must be positive because he was putting you right. The only thing in your mind now is your repaired grip. You can see you have got the left hand positioned precisely as he said, not too much on top. And it feels as he said it should ... golf's a left-hand-dominated game, he said. But that does not mean you should choke the life out of the club. So you are gripping more lightly now; not a lot, but just enough. And you are into your backswing.

Before you have stopped thinking how you were doing everything just the way you had been taught, the ball is flying away ... well, not exactly as you expected. In fact, not very high at all and definitely hooking to the left. Which, considering you positively remembered to do everything you were told, is pretty damn disappointing.

But hardly surprising. Probably the only thing that was right about the swing was the placing and grip of the left hand. Your mind was so dominated by instructions for the left hand, which certainly were very positive, that any good was cancelled out by the negative inference that you were having to remedy a fault. Then there was the total blanking out of any subconscious mechanism to engage your natural swing. With a better hand position and grip integrated with your natural swing pattern, and without negative thoughts about having to put anything to rights, you might have been on the road to recovery.

When first you learn to play golf, and whenever you have remedial treatment for your game, never go straight out and play. When you alter any aspect of your game, make a virtue out of patience, and practise as often as you can. Practise until whatever it is that you have to do that is different is no longer foreign to you. Keep at it for as long as it takes for it to become a natural part of you.

You will have mended your game, and what you will be bringing with you now is not a new model, but the same swing with integral modifications. You will still have your natural swing. Always that will be with you. Its construction may have been slightly modified, but it is still uniquely you and yours and it will come naturally. So you can get up there and subconsciously you can let it happen. And it will.

Providing you have been known to hit, if not perfect strikes, at least good shots, a few times, then it is certain you have a passably good natural swing. Never again must you allow your natural swing to become cluttered with 'how to' thoughts; and do not impede it with doubts about 'what if?' Remember the advice of Scottish professional George Duncan who said: 'The right way to play golf is to go up and hit the bloody thing.' Duncan won the Open at Deal in Kent in 1920 – after two opening rounds of 80 had left him thirteen strokes behind the leader.

So look down at the ball once more; wiggle the clubhead over or behind it if that is what turns you on; start to take the club back . . . and you will be on your automatic subconscious.

TWO

===

NEVER A COPIER BE

I tried to copy 50 other people's swings – and I finally
decided that the best one was my own

Tommy Armour

EVERY GOLFER goes through a round trying to make
copies of something. Whether it is mimicking a favourite
Tour player or attempting to reproduce a copybook
swing by rehearsing over and over in his head all the
rules he can manage to recall from what he has read or
been told about the best way to play the next shot.

Unfortunately, you can never reproduce a perfect
replica even of your own best-remembered golf shot.
You can never create a perfect shot by reciting in your
head all the rules that should (theoretically) bring forth
the miracle. And most of all, you have absolutely no
chance of consciously reproducing that natural ability
which is inborn and which has become, through practice, an inbred and instinctive skill.

What comes naturally comes no other way. You
cannot even produce a deliberately crafted and acceptable copy of your own signature. When you instruct
your mind deliberately to mimic any action that has
been a natural and subconscious part of your make-up
throughout your entire life, even so simple a thing as
your autograph becomes distorted.

The more you are able to appreciate this fact, the better

19

you will be able to accept its significance for your golf game. So take a blank sheet of paper and a pen and in the top third of the page write your signature as you normally would when signing your letters at the office or a cheque at the bank or a credit card voucher at the supermarket. Do not give it a thought, just throw off a signature at the top of the page. Next, scrawl another of your inimitable and possibly indecipherable signatures in the middle of the page.

Now the time has come to put away natural things and give some careful thought to what you are doing. The bottom third of your sheet of paper remains empty. This is where you are going to re-create and reproduce a perfect replica of your signature. The first two thought-less and natural efforts above do have very slight differences, but not markedly so. You might even require a magnifying glass to distinguish between them.

This time, though, you are going to think very hard about what you are doing. You are not going to pen your autograph with a natural flourish. You are going to put time and effort into producing a perfect replica of the one above. You are going to duplicate, slowly and accurately, every variation and blemish, each nuance and idiosyncrasy in your natural signature.

If you really do as we ask, if you try hard to produce a perfect copy, your third 'signature' on the page will be an obvious and, most probably, poor imitation of the natural thing.

If you cannot even make a decent copy of your own signature when you think so hard about doing it, what chance has your natural golf game when you try to encourage it with a selection from your Collected Golf Swings?

Of course we recognize that your natural signature today will be one that has evolved over the years from when you first learned to produce it properly at the age of maybe seven or eight. In the same way, your natural abilities at golf (and the swing is the most fundamental, without which you will not get very far) will have developed and integrated themselves into your highly individual playing personality. Like your own idiosyncratic, natural signature, your golf game is something that not even you, its producer and possessor, are able consciously to imitate. It will have developed and become intrinsic through the passage of time and the hitting of hundreds and thousands and tens of thousands of golf balls. Practice does make perfect on the golf course . . . if you don't think about it.

But every golfer does think about it some of the time. Some of the best players (who might easily be even more successful) appear to think about it all of the time – and particularly when it matters most – when it could determine the result of a tournament that they could so easily win, and when it is therefore most important that they should *not* think about it.

This is the moment when even the most expert and experienced player fails because he has surrendered at the moment when he is most motivated to succeed – and he has surrendered precisely because he is so anxious to achieve success. It is the easiest thing on earth for a prospective champion to miss the winning putt when he switches from the automatic mode that has sunk hundreds (maybe thousands) of more difficult shots.

Although you may do it all time, albeit at a much lower level of both skill and potential glory, perhaps you find it difficult to accept that a top tournament player can miss a gimme on the final green simply because he thinks too much about it. In fact, similar mishaps occur even in the most taken-for-granted actions. As Hans Eysenck, professor emeritus in psychology at the University of London, explains: 'If you think too deeply about the movements in walking down a flight of stairs, you may well finish up in a heap at the bottom!' This is the metaphorical end for many an aspirant sporting champion.

Some never recover from the bad experience. The mental dungeon from which Doug Sanders never escaped was the missed short putt to win the 1970 Open at St Andrews. He had come to the final hole needing a par-4 to win the championship. His approach shot was too strong and he was left with a 30-foot putt down the slope. His putt stopped two feet short of the hole, leaving him one final putt to win the Open. He lined up and then, at the last moment, he leaned forward and removed some tiny obstruction from his line. His nervous jab at the ball forced him into a play-off the next day with Jack Nicklaus – which Sanders lost by one stroke.

Many years later Doug Sanders was asked if the memory of that missed two-footer still haunted him. 'Not as much as it used to,' he replied. 'Sometimes I can go five minutes without thinking about it.'

The failure to pull off the big one at the last hurdle is generally written off as an inability to cope with pressure. In itself the diagnosis is not untrue. But the failure to contend with peak stress has caused the player to choke – he has failed at the most critical moment (perhaps in his entire playing life) to maintain and practise his natural skill.

Scott Hoch, one of the US PGA Tour's outstanding players, a man capable of very low numbers, tied with Nick Faldo in the 1989 Masters Tournament. The sudden-death play-off began on the 10th hole, the 485-yard par-4 Camellia, named like all the Augusta National holes after one of the flowering shrubs which decorate perhaps the best-known golf course in the world. Faldo put his approach shot into a bunker in the middle of the fairway and came out short of the green. Hoch had two putts to win his first major. His first went two-and-a-half feet past the hole. The return putt that would make him Masters Champion was downhill, breaking from left to right.

Just as Sanders had done nineteen years before, Hoch bent down to remove something in front of his ball as he seemed about ready to play. He had spent so much time considering his options that Faldo said later: 'When he took a second look I told myself "Hello . . . this could be interesting!"'

Hoch missed, and Faldo collected the green jacket when he birdied the next.

The danger in switching the emphasis of his game was no less for Scott Hoch than it is for the rest of us. When we have a well established, naturally integrated movement pattern that we have developed over many years, if we shift our whole manner of play from a skill that is executed naturally (and subconsciously) to one where we take over conscious control, then we must expect that the performance will be far less smooth and much less precise.

If a pianist is asked to describe what his hands are doing while he is playing, this will focus his attention on the specific hand and finger movements and his performance will become degraded. On the other hand, when the same pianist is allowed to follow his natural bent and become detached from what his hands are doing, he will produce a superb performance. Victor Borge once knowingly asked a fellow concert great, Vladimir Ashkenazy, in a television chat show: 'Has it ever frightened you to play and watch your fingers moving and not know who it is that is making them move?'

At some stage in every game of golf a player will encounter pressure. For some it may be there only on the first tee, in sight of the clubhouse. For others it may be there on every drive. For most of us, even if we believe we are not prone to pressure, it is certainly there (acknowledged or not) on every gettable putt. And if we are playing competition golf it is there more acutely if we are in contention.

Because there is no question that a breakdown in our ability to play a natural game will be caused by thinking about it too much, it follows that we can avoid disrupting our game style if we know little or nothing about why we play the way we do. Unless and until we have learned to divide our catalogue of dos and don'ts into two categories, one for total and absolute banishment and another for taking out occasionally for the odd brushing up before another period in limbo, then we are better off acquiring as little explicit knowledge as possible about how we exercise whatever skills we possess.

The more prolonged and explicit the instruction we have received in how to execute the skills of golf, the more we have studied the instruction manuals, viewed the videos, consulted the pro, the more certain it is that our natural ability will crumble under every minor stress and strain.

At club level our standard will be diminished even by the small pressures. For some players getting out of a bunker can be more stressful than getting out of a marriage. At the top end of the game, the commercially inspired attempts to nurture the newest graduates of the annual tour qualifying schools prove only that the hit-and-hope method of identifying potentially élite players on the basis of a 108-hole tournament is severely flawed. The long-accepted methods of selection and the subsequent intensive coaching provide a steady stream of volunteers anxious to amass fortunes in the comfort zone of the tours, where money is plentiful but titles few. The winners continue to be drawn from the ranks of those who, knowingly or otherwise, have developed an inner control of their game.

The classic instance of choking, in many other sports as well as in golf, is the situation when a competitor performs outstandingly in practice but poorly in competition. Every golf coach has taught pupils who are capable of striking the ball as sweetly as the best pro in practice but collapse in a competitive situation. The cause was pinpointed more than half a century ago by Sigmund Freud, who suggested that

> . . . many acts are most successfully carried out when they are not the object of particularly concentrated attention . . . mistakes may occur just on those occasions when one is most eager to be accurate.

This is precisely the phenomenon that Tommy Armour was the first to christen 'The Yips'. They plagued his tournament golf through the late 20s and early 30s when he won the US Open, the Open at Carnoustie and the US PGA. After they had driven him out of competitive golf, he wrote: 'The Yips don't seize the victim during a practice round. It is a tournament disease.'

The Yips strike when, under pressure, a player begins to think about how he is implementing his skills. He tries to improve things by recalling to mind, deliberately or otherwise, all the explicit knowledge he has ever imbibed. But if, as we advance from novice to expert status, from unpractised to practised, we can reduce this explicit knowledge to an absolute minimum, then we will have little conscious awareness of the rules which underpin our skills. As a result we will not be able to seek help from a mass of technical know-how in times of stress. What we do not know we know can do us a power of good when the going gets tough on the golf course. Our natural skills will be less likely to break down under pressure, we will be less likely to choke.

Research carried out by Richard Masters at the University of York has shown that (given a basic knowledge of the fundamentals of golf) the less we are instructed and the less technical knowledge we acquire about our own motor skill, the greater is our facility for continuing to develop and improve our natural abilities and to maintain our standard of play under pressure.

Masters based his experiment on the putting green; he could not have controlled his volunteer guinea pigs on a tee or down the fairway, so he chose to subject them to varying conditions of learning and stress on an artificial putting surface which, to make things a little harder, sloped upwards with a gradient of one in four. The research involved forty people, aged between 18 and 46, who were split into five groups of eight, each of which performed under different circumstances. In total, the subjects hit 20,000 putts.

Each group had five practice sessions which took place at the same time on consecutive days, and before each session the volunteers (who performed individually) sat quietly for five minutes to allow their heart rates to settle at base levels. Each of them was paid a set fee and they were all asked neither to think about nor to practise putting while they were away from the experiment.

One group of novices (whom we shall call The Learners) was given very specific written instructions on how to putt, taken from typical golf teaching manuals. It was drilled into them not only that they were expected to read and subsequently re-read these instructions with great care and attention, but also that they should remember to follow them as specifically as possible when they were putting. Thus The Learners were bombarded with the kind of explicit rules that every golfer receives (and which most of them seek out) as long as they play the game.

Another group of novices (The Naturals) was given absolutely no instruction on how to putt. Moreover, any conscious or unconscious attempt which group members might make to develop their own rules was forestalled by obliging them to carry out what in psychology is known as a secondary task. In this case the subjects were required to call out a random letter whenever a metronome clicked. The Naturals were told, quite forcefully, that they must continue to produce these random letters as they putted and that, in fact, they must make it a priority to maintain the randomness of the letters they called out. The other three groups of novices were used as controls, the better to assess the comparative performances of The Learners and The Naturals.

In the early stages of acquiring the skill of putting The Learners (who, like you, the average golfer, had learned many rules) had a level of performance almost as low as that of The Naturals, who had had no putting instruction.

The reason for this superficially surprising result is one you may care (or then again, you may not) to identify with your own experiences. It is reasonable to assume that what limited The Learners' performance was the effort of translating written instructions into physical actions without being given any opportunity for practise. In the same way, and for the same reasons, you will not experience a miraculous recovery of form when you step out onto the course for the first time after a lesson if you have not practised and practised the changes until they have become second nature.

The Learners had been made to study the rules once again before the second day's practice session, but now they were beginning to adjust to the task. They holed almost twice as many putts as on the previous day – an average of 40 out of 100 for each player compared with little more than 20 in the first session. But while The Learners improved by almost 100 per cent, The Naturals were hardly any better than on their first outing, still getting barely more than 20 out of their 100 putts in the hole.

The need to be alert for the next tick of the metronome and to have a random letter ready prevented The

Naturals from devising any rules for playing the shots. It slowed the natural process of acquiring knowledge through practice.

The Learners were getting about one in every two shots in the hole on the third day, and on the fourth day their success rate was unchanged. Meanwhile The Naturals continued to maintain a steady improvement. Now The Naturals were sinking about as many as The Learners. Still neither group was under external pressure, other than that imposed on The Naturals, the only purpose of which was to inhibit their rule-learning mechanism rather than to cause any stress.

But without stress there is no golf; so on the fifth (and final) day the volunteers found themselves under the kinds of stress that the average player experiences every time he goes out and drives to split the fairway, tries to punch a 6-iron within chipping distance, land a pitch shot close to the pin, or putt for a birdie. This time both The Learners and The Naturals were told that the payment originally promised would be increased or decreased – depending upon an evaluation of their final performance by a golf expert.

The suggestion that payments might rise was a ruse to prevent any of the volunteers feeling they had performed so poorly that they might as well make no further effort. To add to the stress the evaluator was introduced to each of the volunteers before they began their final task. Faced with the prospect of their payments diminishing in direct proportion to the number of shots missed (rather like a professional tournament), and under the gaze of a newly introduced expert, all the novices revealed substantially greater anxiety levels and their heart rates increased significantly during the final test.

The big question was whether the putting skills of The Naturals (those who had been given no formal knowledge or rules about how to putt) would withstand the pressure as well as The Learners (who had been instructed in the art). In this final session The Learners were not required to re-read the rules of how to putt and The Naturals were not required to listen for the metronome clicks and recite random letters.

The daily ingestion of the rules over the first four days had left The Learners with a vast repertoire of hints, tips and instructions on how to sink a putt; but under stress they collapsed and their success rate dropped.

The Naturals had shown a steady improvement in terms of the number of shots holed and the upward curve of their results was becoming a little steeper day by day. Now, freed from the artificial distraction of reciting letters, The Naturals stood up under pressure. Indeed in some cases they even improved.

Of course neither group had acquired any real degree of skill at golf. What automatic ability had developed in The Naturals was as primitive in its development as any technically induced skill in The Learners. It takes *at least* ten years to achieve real expertise in a motor skill. (No matter how great the awe in which you hold some of the teenagers at your club, none of them will become real experts for many years.) Nevertheless the experiment proved that the more a golfer's mind is burdened with rules the less well it will perform when the pressure is on: and any of us can be under pressure on the golf course as many times as we have numbers on the day's card.

What is possible in a controlled research environment is not practical on the golf course. We think most golf coaches could do many things very differently; but even so, we recognize they do not have the time or the resources (and certainly not the foresight) to enforce a pattern of implicit learning over all the years it takes any player to become an expert. A much simpler approach would be for all coaches consciously to reduce the emphasis they place on the technical content of the golf skills they are teaching. This would not avoid the problem of players acquiring explicit knowledge (that is a knowledge of the 'how-to' rules) by learning through discovery on the course. But at least this way their deepening pool of explicit knowledge would not be enlarged unnecessarily, as it is today.

Coaches must find a balance between providing a valid and valuable measure of explicit knowledge both at the outset and during a playing life, and encouraging the accumulation of the implicit knowledge that comes only through practice. If a learner holds the wrong end of the club, or stands with his feet together on the tee, then the coach must offer some explicit, technical rules to put him on the right track. How much explicit teaching a coach should give his student depends on the player's innate predisposition to regurgitate such formal knowledge. If the player is what we call a 'low reinvestor' then the coach will know that he can afford to provide more technical detail about the skill than if the student is a 'high reinvestor' who will continually recall all he has ever been told.

In the early 20s the great St Andrews professional Andrew Kirkaldy recorded his memoirs of fifty years in the game. He dictated them to a friend because he could neither read nor write. 'My aim,' he said, 'is to get the learner or medium player into the right frame of mind, with just one or two rock-bottom principles to guide him and not a crowd of ideas to bewilder him.'

Many top performers in all sports execute their skills in ways that are totally different to the stereotype. There was the Borg forehand and the Ali shuffle, and the only reason many of the very best golfers do not add to the deluge of instruction books is that their idiosyncratic styles are not the stuff of which conservative manuals are made. The reason so many top performers in so many sports (though particularly in golf) succeed so consistently is not because their techniques are more effective. Rather it is that their peculiar styles are a part of their natural armoury; they have been developed implicitly rather than explicitly learned. Despite this the (so-called) experts blithely analyse their styles and add their 'secrets' to the instruction manuals before attempting to teach them explicitly to the next generation. This happens in all fields of endeavour. Louis Kentner said it was dangerous to put down cut-and-dried rules of piano playing.

> I have heard pianists who did all the things condemned by everybody else perform miracles of technical perfection. So much depends on imagination, temperament and imponderable things of the mind, and genius often proves that the impossible is the only right solution. There can be no categorical rules and no simple solutions.

Acquiring golf skills (or any other skills) by the implicit learning methods we suggest is not easy in a modern Western culture, where everything from 'politically correct' language to the new season's fashions is codified and where the logical, rational, analytical modes of consciousness are dominant. Explicit knowledge is much easier to deal with and much less subjective.

Moreover, sport imposes its own blocks on implicit learning. Young performers of talent quickly come under enormous pressures to conform to the stereotyped methods of practice that are promoted by all coaches and administrators, by their parents and by their peers. Invariably a young sportsman who is being touted as a coming star or potential champion will have first been noticed at a stage when his performance owed nothing to analytical, logical or explicit rules. But the moment the coaches or the parents begin applying their pressures to practise more, play better, try harder, the 'childlikeness' (as the Zen philosopher Daisetz Suzuki calls it) is destroyed.

Man is a thinking reed but his great works are done when he is not calculating and thinking. 'Childlikeness' has to be restored with long years of training in the art of self-forgetfulness.

Perhaps this is the state that was achieved by Bjorn Borg who claimed that 100 per cent of his game was instinct. 'I never stop and think I'm going to hit a ball cross-court or down the line,' he would say. 'I just do it.'

THREE

════════

THE EMPTY MIND

Like a long-legged fly upon the stream
His mind moves upon silence

W.B. Yeats

HAVING BORROWED or bought his first set of clubs, the beginner is ready to learn what an incredibly complex game he seeks to play. But before even considering the subtleties of the game, he must train his body in the basic motor skills which are fundamental to striking a ball with a club.

There are 792 muscles in the human body, so when you take up any new skill, even the most apparently sedentary, it takes time and much practice to harness the appropriate muscles and co-ordinate them to handle a new task. At first it may seem unbelievably difficult to marshal the vast collection of muscles required to execute even the most gentle swing, and the initial response of the beginner is unconsciously to reduce the number of degrees of freedom he permits his limbs. He locks up a lot of the muscular forces and movements that are required to perform the action; he becomes stiffer and more rigid in order to be able to impose at least some control over his movements.

With practice the body gradually becomes more familiar with what is required and allows the limbs additional degrees of freedom. The movement (for the golfer this is principally the swing) becomes steadily more fluid, the solidity slowly melts away and the stiffness gives way to relaxation. Better still, the player's actions become much more co-ordinated and he begins to hit the ball more sweetly and much further. Without realizing it, he achieves this success by using less, not more, strength.

In any sport, if you begin by holding the club, or the bat, or the cue, or the racket in completely the wrong way, or if you adopt the wrong stance, you will have difficulty hitting the ball correctly. And if you do not hit it correctly you will not hit it a reasonable, let alone a great, distance. For example, it is physically possible to face forwards (rather than sideways-on) and hit a golf ball, but it is not a style that is going to get you anywhere.

In the case of golf, the newcomer needs to spend very little time learning the fundamentals or taking elementary instruction. He needs to know *roughly* how to hold the club (both effectively and, for him, comfortably). He needs to know *roughly* how to stand. He needs to know *roughly* how to swing the club. These few simple things will enable the novice golfer to bring his clubhead down relatively straight and strike the ball cleanly in the right direction. It is not necessary to take the learned fundamentals much further than that.

Most golfers will acquire their first knowledge of how to play the game by going to a club professional. Our own attitudes to professional coaching are not 'Little and Often,' but 'Little and Seldom'. It is vitally important to be ultra-cautious when developing any new motor skill. As we said in the previous chapter, it is too easy for the learner's head to be filled with a catalogue of explicit rules (many of which are quite superfluous to his immediate requirements) that will dog him for the rest of his playing days.

The one constant that unites the tour professional and the everyday golfer is the consuming lust they both have for knowing what they are doing – and how and why they are doing it. Yet, in all sports, when a player produces one of the great performances he will always (not often, but *always*) admit, if subsequently asked, that he can hardly remember what he was doing.

When he was number one in the tennis world, Stefan Edberg came off court after one of those days when he had played almost perfect tennis.

> In the third set I started to think a little bit and wondered if it was a dream. So I said to myself: 'Just keep concentrating on each point.' If you start to think you can easily get into trouble.

When Martina Navratilova won her famous victory in the 1987 French Open she said: 'I played for an hour and I don't think I missed a shot. Everything was happening without me having to think.'

It is possible to immerse yourself in what the Americans call 'The Zone' – not thinking about technique, not worrying about the rules which tell you how to play the stroke – even when you are gambling with something more important than a transitory glory. The Spanish bullfighter Juan Belmonte said of the fight that made him a legend:

> . . . all at once I forgot the *aficionados*, the *toreros*, myself – even the bull. I simply fought as I believe one ought to fight. Without a thought – outside my own faith in what I was doing.

It was not fear for his personal safety that drove any thoughts from the matador's mind. The same thing happened on the squash court to British champion Lisa Opie, who does not remember a thing about the best match she ever played. It was in the world team championships in New Zealand. Great Britain was one-love down in the series and Opie was playing the Australian Vicki Cardwell, four times British Open champion. She recalls:

I might remember the first service but that's all. I was in a trance of concentration, a cocoon of invincibility. I came off the court, and I didn't have a clue about the score – except that I beat her. You play by instinct, by auto-pilot. And you win famously. It's uncanny.

When Lee Janzen won the US Open at Baltusrol in 1993, Jack Nicklaus talked of how he was 'in a zone of his own. He's oblivious to everything that's happening around him.' And Amy Alcott compares playing good golf on the women's tour in America to a religious experience: 'I get very quiet and I go into a zone where I don't see things, and people talk but I don't hear what they're saying.'

But for every top performer who achieves his or her greatness within The Zone there are many more who fall to pieces outside it. Those who succeed beyond anyone's expectations, who play beyond themselves, are not focusing conscious attention on the act they are performing. Turning inwards what Boris Pasternak called 'The beam of consciousness' while performing a highly skilled action can be catastrophic. Pasternak had Dr Zhivago advise Anna Ivanovna Gromeko that

> . . . trying consciously to go to sleep is a sure way to have insomnia. To try to be conscious of one's own digestion is a sure way to upset the stomach. Consciousness is a poison when we apply it to ourselves. Consciousness is a beam of light directed outwards, it lights up the way ahead of us so that we don't trip up. It's like the headlamps on a railway engine – if you turned the beam inwards there would be a catastrophe.

Scott Hoch would have had tummy rumblings certainly after (and probably during) his missed gimme in the Masters. Similarly that most clinical of snooker players, Steve Davis, was only too conscious of the do-or-die situation he was in when he missed the final black of the final frame to lose the world championship in 1986.

Golfers have been, and still are, made far too aware of the complexities of the game and give too much attention to trying to analyse their own skills. The few players on the Tour who talk to sports psychologists do so not because they want to empty their minds of unnecessary rules so they can be their own selves in their play, but rather because they feel a need to conform to the modern mania for counselling. Many of them appear to be anxious to unburden their souls, very few of them are prepared to unburden their minds. And the advisers who are content to console their clients by urging them to focus their minds on thinking positively are no better than quacks dispensing sugar pills in place of cures.

It is impossible to review mentally a whole set of rules in the two seconds it takes to hit a golf ball. Yet too many professionals try to do this. When Seve Ballesteros had listened to all those whose advice he asked, plus those who dared venture it, and after he had escaped from a brief sojourn with master guru David Leadbetter in the early part of 1994, he found a new swing doctor, Mac O'Grady. Not the least idiosyncratic of the American Tour's performers, 'Mad Mac' as he is (kindly) known, passed on to Ballesteros forty 'neuro-scientific' changes to his game make-up, the fruits of his 'ten-year study of the golf swing'.

Ballesteros, who has contributed so much to golf, unintentionally did it a great disservice when he confidently claimed to be able to remember 38 of the 40 rules O'Grady laid down. Taken at face value, which is how the *aficionados* take the wisdom of their heroes, the Spaniard's example would lead millions of average golfers throughout the world to assume that they should walk out to the first tee reciting a litany of rules to themselves.

Of course Ballesteros was not consciously exaggerating his powers of recall; innocently, but inaccurately, he was trying to explain his new facility. But no-one, not even Ballesteros, is capable of processing 38 thoughts in the course of a two-second swing. Whether or not he realized it, he had incorporated those new rules into his mental programmer, so that they had become a part of his natural game, leaving only two of the things O'Grady Says to think about. As Ballesteros's game slowly began to creep back to something approaching recognizable form, he had got himself to within two thoughts of recovery – two thoughts away from an empty mind.

For the ideal state of mind at the moment of play is one without even a single thought. An empty mind.

You may not have realized this before, but if you think about it now, you have probably achieved this ideal state when you have been trying to put some change into your own swing. Some of your attempts will have produced no improvement, some will have resulted in worse shots, but there will have been the odd occasion when it all came together. Your partner may have reminded you what you were trying to do only seconds before you swung, and yet, when it worked, you may have thought to yourself how strange that it came off just when you had not even given it a thought. In future you might think it's not so strange at all. So we say to you once again: Forget it. Play with an empty mind.

Ben Crenshaw is loved both by his fans and his peers as much as he loves the traditions of the game he has adorned. When he is not playing golf, or designing courses, or collecting golf artifacts, he listens to country and western or goes fishing or bird-watching. Or he speaks gentle words of wisdom:

> It is difficult to explain to someone how fragile the difference is in professional golf between good and great, between winning and finishing tenth. It is actually infinitesi-

mal. The difference, when there are so many at the same skill level, is an uncluttered mind.

We take things a stage further than Ben Crenshaw. We say good golf demands the ultimate – a mind that is filled with nothing.

This is the most difficult golf lesson you will ever be required to learn. If you persevere and succeed it will also be the most rewarding. It will enable you to play to the best of your natural ability. It may make you consistently good or it may make you consistently average-to-middling, but the next best thing to greatness is consistency. It may not lead to triumph, but it avoids disappointment.

You will need tuition in the fundamentals of golf, but it is vital not to get carried away. Learn only the basics. If you have the basics and if you can go out on the course and hit no more than one or two good shots in a round (whether or not you are a total beginner), what is the point of saying to yourself: 'Hang on here – I've got to improve my basic skill.'? If you start to think like this you will start to copy and your golf will start to look like your copied signature. Learn to go out there and just do it.

How often have you come across someone who has just taken up a new sport and proved to be incredibly good at it – yet they will swear that they have never done it before? It is quite extraordinary how often people (and not only young people) will produce a phenomenally good performance the first time they practice a new skill. But after that first attempt, if left to themselves without even the most elementary guidance in the basics, their performance disintegrates.

What has happened is that they have initially 'had a go' with the innocence of the uninitiated, without any attempt to be analytical and without a head full of rules. They have done it without thinking about how to do it. The next time they go out they try to match the standard which they set for themselves at their first attempt; they try to remember how they did it, and they try to repeat their actions. They recall when it felt good and they say to themselves: 'I must try to do that again.' The result is that they fall apart – and cannot understand why.

If only there was a way of maintaining the state of innocence which is the explanation of 'beginner's luck'. The state in which the mind has no memories of a previous outing, no models to copy, no rules to try to remember.

Unfortunately you cannot put someone on to the golf course and tell him: 'Off you go then – and remember, don't you dare even think about any of those rules that tell you how to play.' You can't stop him recalling the rules he has read, or been told, or discovered for himself. For even if he is not given any rules to start with, he will soon start making up his own. Nonetheless, we have to discourage golfers from building up a list of how-to-play rules once they have mastered the basics. This is made even more difficult than it need be because all sport (golf being typical) is practised, at the lower levels, in the shadow of the numerous popular heroes created by the media.

The newcomer (and the not-so-newcomer) will model his skills on the likes of a Faldo, a more rules-orientated player than whom it is impossible to imagine. Difficult though it is to persuade seasoned golfers that emulation is a giant step towards immolation, lesser mortals must be made to practise becoming their own true selves rather than flawed copies of what, after all, are not necessarily the best examples.

The best way to free yourself from the compulsion to be bound by rules is to think back to the last really good shot you played, or the best one you have ever played. We promise it will have been a shot you just *played*. Just like that. You did not think how to hit it as you swung at it. You did it without reciting to yourself the rules of engagement. The best shots you will ever play in future will be those you hit without giving them a thought.

Now you know how the empty mind really works. But you do not know how to produce an empty mind; and we cannot tell you how to clear out all your mental debris. What we can do is to suggest some methods that will put you on the road to achieving the desired state. In the end though it has to be up to you, and only you.

To appreciate how difficult it is to empty your mind completely, look at your watch and follow the second-hand for ten seconds. Programme your mind to think about nothing for those ten seconds. It's not a long time. Ten seconds is nothing when you measure it against the four hours of an average round of golf. After the ten seconds have gone, recall all the things you *did* think about. Of course, you did not empty your mind at all, did you? It's not even empty when you are asleep.

While the ideal remains a completely empty mind, a mind which hears no swing-thoughts, does not imagine it can see swing-images, and does not strive to take control of your natural swing, there are one or two ways of creating an *almost* empty mind. This is not to compromise nor to concede the impossibility of creating the perfect state of mind. It is simply to play the mind-game as you should play your entire golf game – by making the best out of whatever you've got.

If you cannot conjure up an empty mind, you must make it as difficult as possible for unwanted thoughts to creep in. Try to focus on only one thing when you are swinging through the ball. Block out all the other rules by giving the mind a master thought, a Thought for the Day.

This thought that you are going to think every time you swing in the course of a round may be something that you have found useful in improving your game in the past. You may use the same thought every time you play or you may care to draw up a list of helpful hints

41

and extract different ones for different rounds. Whatever thought you pick on will turn off all the other thoughts. No matter how helpful the one thought may be, its primary purpose is to block out all the others and bring you as close as possible to the ideal of a totally barren psyche.

You can use the one-thought rule to good effect when you have just been to the pro and you go out to play, with your mind full of his shopping list of rules. Nick Price was a David Leadbetter pupil when he won both the Open and the US PGA championships in 1994. But their coaching sessions were separated by several weeks and each time Price looked for just the one thought to help him. 'Once David has struck a chord I don't want to hear any more,' he explains. 'That's quite enough until the next time.' Price concedes that Nick Faldo is different and can stand constant tinkering with his game. 'He wants to know if this is right and then that and then something else,' he says. 'But it is very unusual to be able to absorb all those things and then actually go out and win.'

It is perfectly understandable, when you go to the pro and pay for his advice, that he should recognize his responsibility to give his client value for money. And, no doubt, you expect value for your money. Both of you can be satisfied in one of two ways. If you go away and find that you are playing better, of course you will be satisfied, and the pro will feel he has fulfilled his part of the bargain. Equally, if you go away with a whole list of new dos and don'ts you will feel you have got your money's worth and the pro will conclude that as he has been able to diagnose so many minor faults, and to suggest so many ways of rectifying them, he must have given you what you paid for.

Alas, it is not that simple. When Richard Masters visited the pro for the first time, he had been playing golf for five years, he had never had a lesson and he was playing off eight. He sought advice because for some time he had been fading the ball, almost slicing his drives. Although he realized that he should have accepted this as his natural shot (which, of course, it was) he decided, partly in the interests of research, to assume that there must be something wrong with a fundamental skill which required the pro's attention.

So, complying with the principle that a visit to the swing-doctor can be justified when one of the fundamentals of the natural swing seems to have broken down, he sought professional assistance and was rewarded with half-a-dozen or so pointers. When he was let loose again on the fairways he was confronted with the problem of how to handle six or seven new swing-thoughts. He could hardly remember them all, and it was certainly impossible to put them all into effect at the same time.

So he tried to find one thought that would encompass all the new rules; so that he could stand up to the ball, think of that one thing and banish everything else from his mind. The pro had told him that his divots were pointing the wrong way (inside the line of the ball), his club was coming from outside the ball (so sliding across the face of the ball and slicing), his hips were turning too early and his shoulder was coming up and what he needed to do was to have his hips and his legs and his body going directly along the line of the ball and that this would bring the clubhead cleanly behind the ball at impact...

Masters told himself that, technically, the pro was right. He accepted that the professional had diagnosed something that was wrong with the fundamentals of his swing. What could he do that would achieve the aim of all his new rules combined (some remembered, others forgotten) without blocking up his head? He decided that if he kept his hip pointing where the ball was intended to go for as long as he could, that would achieve what he sought. And indeed it does.

He now has one Thought for the Day: he is going to keep his hip from turning. The effect of this limited thinking is of course that his hip turns after the strike, but not so early as before when he was fading and slicing. And he is not thinking of anything else. He has an almost empty mind.

When you start to worry about a bad shot all the rules that say how it should and could have been played will flood into your head; and the first thing that has to be done before you can make the next shot any better is to flush them all out again. The next thing, with a clear head and no thought – either of rules or memories of what just happened – is to find a friend.

Wherever your ball lies as a result of that troubling bad shot, take no account of difficulty or distance – go to your bag and take out your favourite club, the one you have always hit pretty well most of the time you have been playing the game. Provided you are still approaching the green it can be any club apart from the putter. For most golfers it will be their 5-iron.

Even if your favourite is a pitching wedge, with which you normally hit no more than 100-yards at best, go back to it for a couple of shots. If you are on a long par-4 tell yourself that perhaps you are not going to make it in two but that you will get there in three, and may still have a choice of knocking a putt in or chipping and putting for a five. Very often you will surprise yourself and get close in two and make par.

By using your favourite club which, by definition, is also the one with which you are the most confident, you are less likely to be filling your head with ideas and rules and all those unwanted swing-thoughts. Better still, you will not be remembering the last shot that did not come off.

And you will be getting closer to an empty mind.

FOUR

===

ROUTINE MATTERS

Perfection consists not in doing extraordinary things, but in doing ordinary things extraordinarily well

Angèlique Arnauld

THE PUNISHMENT for one bad shot in a round of golf can often be disproportionate to the reward provided by any number of good shots; and the vagaries of the game can cause even the best golfer in the world to mis-hit frequently. If a man of such practised consistency as Tom Kite can hit an air-shot, how can the club golfer, who hits fewer balls in a year than Kite hits in a week, expect not to make mistakes a-plenty?

Mistakes occurring on the golf course may be attributable either to external distractions (things going on around us that disturb our concentration) or to internal distractions (things going around in our head that disturb our mental focus); on top of which there is *stress*. If you dislike that word because of its modern connotation of instability, you may seek to minimize it and call it pressure; but whatever the cause of your mis-hits, there are ways of reducing the number you are likely to make in any round. The pre-shot routine is a sure way of helping every golfer play fewer bad shots.

In most sports it takes some time to warm up and achieve a normal level of performance, and in many sports this is no problem. If you lose the first three points at squash or perhaps the first (or even the second) game, all is not lost. You still have a chance to get back into contention. In golf, you have only to hook your first shot out of bounds and before you know where you are you have taken eight.

In no other sport is it possible to play the very first shot of the game without any warm-up – and to be punished so harshly for a mistake that it can ruin your whole game. The pressure is always greatest on the first shot because it is the most public shot you will play. The first tee is usually in view of the clubhouse, and often of the congregation outside the pro's shop. Enthusiasts on the practice green close by pay more heed to drives off the first tee than they do to their own putts, and the trolley path towards the first tee regularly contains a queue of interested spectators. It is not until he has driven off the first that the average club golfer is able to relax slightly and contemplate the fickleness of his chosen avocation.

A mandatory warm-up period is written into the rules of many sports. In professional tennis, players are allowed a five-minute warm-up, and amateurs have their knock-up, too. Squash players are allowed three minutes to tune up, physically and mentally. Golfers do not get this opportunity. The first hole stands substitute. If only we were allowed to go back and play it again!

The *pre-shot* routine is not to be confused with a *pre-match* routine or with any ritual that may be practised in the lengthy gaps between shots.

A pre-match routine is something which is performed well before the event begins. Touring professionals have evolved such (generally subconscious) routines over several years; and thought out or not, the pro's pre-match routine will be a little more formalized than that of the amateur. But even so, most golfers – were they to see themselves as others see them – would recognize that when preparing to leave for the club they do the same things, at the same stage, in the same way, in the same order, at the same speed. Things like dusting off the clubs, putting them in the right compartments in the bag, checking bag pockets for pencils, tee pegs, markers, and all the other things they are anxious not to forget. And every golf bag that ever was is borne from its sanctum in the same manner and reverently laid in car boot in precisely the same way every time it leaves home. Think about it!

The pre-shot routine is something which you only perform just before you hit the ball, before you hit every ball in every game. What goes on in those gaps between shots is a matter of personal preference. Talk with your partners about your boss or your wife (if the two are distinguishable). Laugh about them (if you can). Enjoy the enforced break in the rhythm of striking at balls by talking of other things, of shoes and string and sealing wax, if you must – anything but that last shot going wrong. Even if it was good, the next shot is something else altogether.

Among modern-day golfers Lee Trevino is perhaps the best example of a man who keeps his playing problems at bay by talking away his tensions, talking to his playing partners if they will listen, to the fans if they are in earshot, or, quite happily, to himself. He was partnered by Tony Jacklin in one world match play when Jacklin told him he did not want to talk. 'Okay with me,' replied Trevino. 'Just listen!' Whatever he has concocted for his pre-shot routine (Trevino's entire game is self-made) his soliloquy often continues through his backswing and sometimes beyond.

The master of manipulating the moments between shots was Walter Hagen. When he won his first Open Championship at Royal St George's in 1922 he gave his £50 cheque to his caddie but cashed in on this, the first of his four British Open titles, by showing his contemporaries and successors how to make a million away from the course. On it he showed us how to spend our time between shots. 'Don't hurry. Don't worry,' he said. 'You're only here on a short visit, so don't forget to stop and smell the roses.' His pre-tournament routine consisted of late night bridge, champagne and cigars, whisky and women. He never arrived on the first tee before his opponent and as he strolled out he would drawl: 'Waal, who's gonna be second?' According to Henry Longhurst, he made more bad shots winning every one of his eleven majors than the runner-up would make in a month. His powers of recovery were almost superhuman – and so was his philosophy.

Unlike their less rewarded but more exalted forebears, today's touring professionals are idolized by millions of could-have-been-contenders who are brainwashed by the golfing establishment (and a consenting media) into believing they are seeing the greatest. In fact, today's top pros have put only eight yards onto the average drive over the past quarter of a century and overall scores have improved by only a stroke or two between 1969 (when, for example, George Archer won the Masters with 281) and 1994 (when José Maria Olazabal had 279). Nick Faldo won his first green jacket in 1989 with 283 – just one shot better than Horton Smith had taken to become the first Masters champion 55 years earlier.

Despite this evidence that today's players have taken the game to some kind of natural limit, dedicated achievers like Faldo do not accept that the kind of barrier that exists in every other sport applies in golf. Most professionals – and very many competition-conscious low-handicap players – desperately seek help as they see this barrier towering just ahead of them. Frank Thomas, technical director of the United States Golf Association, says a lot of them turn to the latest in high-tech equipment, like $500-plus clubs. Some of them actually begin to see a genuine improvement in their performance, but, says Thomas, this is 'only a psychological boost and it wears off after a time.'

What does not wear off after any length of time is a well-ordered, programmed and relaxed mind. The pre-shot routine is an invaluable, and at the same time a simple, means of realizing this happy state.

Players like Faldo and Colin Montgomerie have their own individualistic pre-shot routines that they believe work for them. But in neither case do their routines satisfy one of our three principal requirements for any pre-shot routine – they do not prevent them being distracted by external happenings on the course.

Surprisingly, Faldo seems less disturbed by the bellowing of his major-domo caddie, Fanny Sunesson, exhorting miscreants among his fairway followers to 'Stand still . . . Please!' or proclaiming 'No cameras!' than he is by the actual movements among his fans or the stuttering of their shutters. Though he may not realize it, her incantations can only fuel his distractions. Having already allowed himself to be disturbed by the cameras, he can only be further distracted by her concern for her master's peace of mind.

Colin Montgomerie is as much a perfectionist as Faldo, though less obsessively so. Often he has seemed uncertain whether his role is Crown Prince or Clown Prince. When he went out to Corey Pavin in the semi-final of the 1993 World Match Play Championship he first hurled a ball onto the green in disgust, and then dented a tee by slamming his driver into the ground. Later he kicked his putter and then his bag. After lunch he three-putted the 5th and then screamed 'No cameras – Christ Almighty!' after his drive on the 7th tee. Afterwards Montgomerie complained: 'People should not bring cameras. One out of three people had them out there and it affected my concentration. It's not for me to learn not to be distracted. It's for people to learn to stop bringing cameras to tournaments.'

Twelve months after uttering this immortal soundbite, which we shall analyse for the benefit of lesser mortals in a moment, Montgomerie had embarked upon an image clean-up campaign and did admit during the English Open that he 'must learn to be patient and stay in control'.

Whatever Montgomerie's eventual contribution to world golf, his World Match Play solipsism will remain the most eloquent endorsement of the value of a good pre-shot routine. If his routine had been effective in keeping his mind focused on the next shot he would not have been so distracted from his game as to be able to calculate the proportion of camera-wielding fans. It was not the fans that distracted him, it was his insistence on worrying about something he saw as a problem which created the distraction. And he really has it all wrong if he believes that he ought not to learn not to be distracted.

There will always be potential distractions of one kind or another for every golfer at every hole in every game on every course. The fans with their cameras are the *raison d'être* of the PGA tours, they are as much a part of a competition player's life as the falling leaves in the rough or the pounding waves by the links.

Most golfers, if they even know what a pre-shot routine is, imagine it to be some sort of ritualistic affectation unique to touring professionals – not something that the average club player should consider to be as intrinsic a part of the swing as the grip or the stance. In fact, the pre-shot routine is a necessary ingredient in any recipe for a good game of golf. It is not something that demands an effort on your part, but an action that will become as natural a part of your golfing make-up as the swing itself. In return for the minimal effort it demands it will massage away the mental and the physical aches in your game that are caused by those inevitable inactive delays between shots. It will be the best facilitator you are likely to find to help you towards that ideal of an empty mind or (as a close-run second-best) having that single, simple Thought for the Day.

The pre-shot routine is something you must go through before every single shot. Its basis will be the same each time, though you may vary it for different situations and, of course, your routine before putting will not be quite the same as before teeing-off.

If you start thinking yourself into your routine as you select your club, you will automatically slide into it. The constituent parts will be executed as meticulously and precisely as anything you could have drilled into you at Sandhurst or West Point. You may, for example, decide always to approach the ball from behind, because that way you will see the target line best; at this point you may interpose some practice swings, but because the golf swing relies heavily on muscle memory, beware of the practice swing that might be less than perfect. When you come to the real thing a few moments later, your muscles might remember the practice.

So, you have moved around to the address position and you will find that you settle into it the same way every time – if you start with your feet together and then move the right foot to the side, that is the way it will always be. If you place the clubhead square behind the ball in line with the target before you adjust your feet, always do this. If you keep the clubhead an inch or so above the ground before a slight lunge forward to ground it as you are initiating your swing, then never ever touch the ground before that moment in future. If you normally look at the ball and then up and left toward the target three times before swinging, never look at the target twice or four times. If your particular idiosyncrasy is to waggle the clubhead as if you were bullying off on the hockey field, then you will always tap the ground behind your ball and then your imaginary opponent's non-existent stick a regular number of times. If you are a proper sporting pedant you will, of course, do this three times.

Do whatever you want to do and do it your own way. Shuffle your feet, waggle your club, cock your head, twist your body – but do it consistently. The set-up is the only aspect of the swing over which you should have one hundred per cent conscious control. That means you must have a routine that is not 'almost exactly' the same every time, but *always* the same in its basics, varied only by the demands of the ball's lie or the differing demands of a drive off the tee, or of a bunker shot, or of a putt. Your performance will be unchanging and the speed at which you go, from selecting your club to swinging through the ball, should never vary by more than the odd second. Your pre-shot routine should not be hurried, but it should not be slow or laboured. If it flows smoothly it will dictate its own pace and slide smoothly into your swing.

The beauty of the pre-shot routine is that it is neither difficult nor complicated. It demands very little mental effort and no real physical exertion. Quite simply, it offers you the ideal way to stop your mind from wandering after the mental and physical pauses between shots. It will stop you focusing on how you are going to execute this next shot, on what the rules may say for getting out of this position, on how you are going to get the ball into the air or into the hole. The pre-shot routine will keep out all those internal distractions, all those thoughts about what happens if you get this one wrong. And it will prevent you from being put off (or even, like some, becoming mentally unhinged for a moment) by irrelevant external disturbances. Additionally, but also very importantly, it will help you to cope with those extra-pressure shots that crop up in every round of golf.

If you have a proper pre-shot routine you will not suffer from the distractions of other people moving when you are about to strike, or be put off by the horsefly nestling in the first dimple below the second letter of the maker's name on the ball, or be disturbed by the noise of cars and planes, or the talk and loud laughter coming from adjoining fairways.

Another enormous benefit of the pre-shot routine is that it brings the player's attention back into focus. In golf there is a gap between every single shot – some times as much as ten or more minutes may pass by as you wait on the tee for the group ahead to move on after their second shots. Where the squash player may suffer what the scientists call 'warm-up decrement' between sets, the golfer has to counter scores of attacks of warm-up decrement in every round by finding a way to re-establish a proper state of mind and body in order to achieve his natural performance level. No matter what his normal standard of play, he has to spend a short time before every shot getting back onto a plane from which he may not realize he has slipped.

The pre-shot routine is an invaluable means of achieving this. It will prime you for every shot you play; it will make you both mentally and physiologically ready to perform close to your best with very little effort. In short, the pre-shot routine is a way of responding correctly to the new challenge of the next shot.

Few golfers are able to head for the locker room confident that not one shot they have played that day has been affected by some internal or external distraction, or by some pressure (they will not like to call it stress), or by too much confused thinking. Most would have to admit that many, perhaps all, of their shots have been influenced to some degree by one, or even a combination, of these factors. The pre-shot routine will change this for ever. If you adopt a pre-shot routine today you will find yourself playing your very next game unhampered by many of the interfering thoughts that have troubled you since your first lesson all those years ago.

The first requirement of the pre-shot routine is that it should be consistent. After all, we want to achieve the same result every time we hit a ball. John Burns remembers seeing the best demonstration of the benefits of a consistent pre-shot routine coming from Ray Floyd in 1986, not long after he had become (at the age of 43) the then oldest winner of the US Open Championship. He had just gone through his regular pre-shot routine before a 180-yards approach shot. As he was about to launch into his backswing a figure dashed across the fairway in front of the green. Some players would have continued with the strike, some might have exploded in anger at the distraction, others might have stepped back a pace and then returned to the address and gone on from there. But not Floyd. He walked away from the ball and handed his club back to his caddie who returned it to the bag. Floyd waked away from the bag, turned and walked back to it. He selected the same club, drew it out of the bag, re-enacted his entire pre-shot routine, and landed the ball on the green.

A pre-shot routine is a simple thing to devise. You can be developing your own right now as you read this, or you can think about it and put it together the next time you are out on the course. It takes only a little time to prepare, and a short time to perform. Whether you realize it or not, before you come to the end of this chapter you will have put together a mental image of your own pre-shot routine. It will be clear in your head when you lay down the book or when you next prepare to strike a ball. But when you run through it for the first time, remember that from then on you are going to go through this rigmarole (or a very similar one) every time you hit a golf ball. The pre-shot routine will help you cope with stress on the golf course in the same way that a 'pre-drive' routine helps you get underway when you are in a rush every morning.

Imagine: you are late for work as usual, you have to

back out onto a busy main road and you have to be out and moving forward again before being hit by that big truck you see bearing down on you. You may never have realized that you are under a great deal of stress doing this everyday thing so early in the day. Nor will you have realized that you engineer it so smoothly because you employ a natural, automatic pre-drive routine in order to accomplish it without being distracted by any of the manifold goings on in the street. Reversing out onto the main road with its inherent dangers is like putting to save or win the match. Without your pre-emptive routines you will probably miss the putt or stall the car.

The reason you do not stall the car, even though you are an experienced and (you think) expert driver, is that you have denied yourself the worry and the added stress of focusing on irrelevant things by performing (naturally and automatically) your own pre-drive routine. You have not been distracted by the neighbour encouraging his dog to foul the footpath opposite your driveway. You have not given way to the temptation to think about the consequences of not getting backed out before that truck gets here – such thoughts may not be entirely irrelevant in life's order of things but (in perspective) they are irrelevant and would distract you from the established and secure performance of your driving skill.

Of course we have no idea what your pre-drive routine may be. But if you think about it you will realize that you do the same things in the same order and at the same speed every time you drive out. Key, clutch, handbrake, ignition, mirror, signal, reverse gear, accelerator and so on. You may do these things automatically now, but at least part of your driving routine will have evolved from conscious learning of the Highway Code. This pre-drive routine is the preamble to executing the skill of reversing the car onto a busy main road and driving away without allowing any external or internal distractions to lead you into danger. Some thoughts of the problems involved in driving in the rush hour may have passed through your mind, but as you were naturally going through your automatic and subconscious pre-drive routine you did not focus on them.

When you are standing over a three-foot putt on the golf course the consequences of the strike you are about to perform will be in the forefront of your mind, so much so that they will almost certainly affect your putt – unless you have a pre-shot routine. Bobby Locke used to take a couple of practice swings, one pace forward, one look at the hole – and away the ball went for better or worse; usually better.

Whenever you are under pressure, on or off the golf course, it becomes very difficult to control your mind. Your thoughts jump all over the place. They flit illogically from one thing to another. They will not sit still. Probably your heart will begin pounding as well. Your mouth may go dry. It may be a difficult thing to do, but you have got to take yourself in hand. Instinctively you take a deep breath because you believe this will help to calm you down. Often it takes a long time, but it does work.

Try to think of the pre-shot routine as rather like a rock to which you must cling. Get a firm grip and it will help you focus on what is relevant rather than on what is irrelevant – such as that terrible last shot you played. It prevents your thoughts fluttering around. Many times you must have found yourself walking down the fairway after a fantastic drive that has gone clean down the middle – the kind of shot that even British commentators nowadays call 'Position "A"'. There are only two holes to play. You think: 'That's great. I've got par made on this hole. All I have to do is par the next and I've done my best score ever.' What do you do? You go up to the ball, you attack it . . . and you duff it.

Instead of telling yourself only about the shot you are about to play, you have been assuming that you have already parred this hole. You should have been thinking exclusively of the shot you were about to play, but you have not focused on it at all. If you had approached the ball and gone through your pre-shot routine, read off to yourself a kind of checklist that would have brought your mind back to the current shot and eliminated all memories of the previous shot or worries about the next hole, then you would have got all the irrelevant thoughts out of your head and you would have played a more effective shot.

Try to think of your pre-shot routine as a shopping list of the things you need to do in order to prime your mind and body to play the best shot you possibly can. When you begin to think how you will construct your own routine, do not rush off to hire a video of The Masters or The Open and try to copy the pre-shot routines of the rich and famous. They may not work properly for them, let alone for you. Pre-shot routines differ from player to player; they are as bespoke as a Savile Row suit. And just as you would not queue for the Hard Rock Café in the same gear you would choose for lunch at the Savoy Grill, you will have a pre-shot routine that varies slightly according to the shot in prospect.

Your routine may be as individualistic and eccentric as you wish, though perhaps not so peculiar as that practised by Turk Wendell, pitcher for the Greenville Braves in the United States Southern Baseball League. He starts his routine by crossing the foul line with a three-foot kangaroo leap; then he circles the mound (always anticlockwise) and walks to the rubber and squats – if the catcher is squatting, then he must stand; if the catcher will not stand, Wendell stands. The next stage in his ritual is to walk off the mound, look to centrefield, say a prayer and cross himself. Then he points to the centrefielder, who must wave back. Finally Wendell draws three crosses in the dirt behind the rubber and then licks the dirt from his fingers.

What we now offer you is a potpourri of some of the ingredients that you can incorporate into your basic all-shots routine. But first let us caution you not to think of the pre-shot routine as a substitute for the ideal of the empty mind or, the next-best thing, a single Thought for the Day – in fact the final stage of the routine should be the emptying of your mind or, if you can't achieve that, concentrating your thoughts on that single idea.

Your routine should be simple: not too long, not too complicated, not too difficult to remember. Make it a sequence which will form a natural and automatic part of your golf psyche, a process to be set in motion by rote as you approach every future shot. It should incorporate all the vital components of your game.

You will realize by now that your mis-hits are always going to outnumber your perfect strikes. So it makes sense to minimize the damage in advance. To accept this is not to be guilty of negative thinking. The negative thought that does the damage is the one we indulge in immediately before we hit the ball. Here we are planning the very first thought we shall have as we start our pre-shot routine.

As you come up to your lie, start by asking yourself: 'If I get it wrong, where *don't* I want the ball to end up?' Say that you are nicely positioned well down the centre of the fairway, and you have a good approach shot to the green. On the left, just in front of the green, is a large bunker. If you hit slightly left you will be in the hazard or you will need to play a really tricky shot over the bunker to get onto the green. Over on the right it is flat and safe and if you come up short you will have a comfortable little chip or you might even be able to putt the ball on. So the first thing you will do as you launch into your pre-shot routine is to say to yourself: 'If I get this wrong and miss the green, where *do* I want to be?' You are not saying, 'I hope I don't go into the bunker' or 'I mustn't land it there.' In effect you are telling yourself that you must go for the flag, but if you miss you are going to miss on the right.

This kind of self-counselling (much preferable, we think, to the one-on-one soul-searching that is a growing feature of the major tours) is useful before every shot. It does not play one shot ahead, but it does pave the way for an easier shot to follow.

Now you might like to look at your set-up – your grip and your stance. For many golfers the major problem with the stance is lining up properly. So in developing your routine it is important to figure out a way which will allow you to have yourself lined up correctly in as short a time as possible and with the least amount of trouble – and then forget about it.

Some coaches suggest pretending to shoot a rifle or a shotgun. They say you should take the golf club and hold it to your shoulder like a marksman, pointing at the target. Traditionalists say that an imaginary line from right toe through left toe should run parallel to the line from ball to target. Others prefer to sight the target through a marker such as a weed or distinctive tuft of grass a few feet ahead of the ball.

When you use your pre-shot routine you are neatly arranging the mechanical parts of the swing process. Even more importantly, you are manning the defences of your mind against the onslaught of irrelevant and unnecessary thoughts and repelling distractions that will catch your attention if you leave room in your mind to accommodate them. This means that your pre-shot routine should fully occupy your attention from the moment you begin to prepare your shot until the start of the backswing.

During this time – in the build-up period before striking the ball – your body will be undergoing a change, through its own volition. And if only you were able to monitor what was going on you would know beforehand whether you were going to hit a good one. Because if it is to be a successful shot the electrical activity in the brain will have reduced to a minimum and the heartbeat will have slowed. If the heart rate has gone up, the chances of a good shot will have gone down. This slowing of the heartbeat always occurs immediately before you play a natural, unforced stroke. Why this should happen is something of a mystery, but it is known that it is associated with an increased focus of attention, along with a relaxed concentration. And the two extremes of this paradox – profound attention and greater relaxation – come only from allowing the skill to be performed automatically and naturally.

Inhaling or exhaling and then holding the breath can encourage the stillness of mind and the relaxation of the body that generally precede any competent act. It is a *sine qua non* for the rifleman and the archer that they hold their breath at the moment of shooting. Generally this has been thought to be a device merely to encourage a physical steadiness, which is even more important for the marksman than the golfer. In fact, squeezing the trigger or striking the golf ball between breathing out and breathing in (or the other way around if you prefer) helps us concentrate on just one thing. It makes us better able to disregard the distractions which will deflect our aim. Holding one's breath may encourage cardiac deceleration which in turn reduces the feedback of information to the brain . . . and we all know that the less information that gets through, the more chance we have of approaching the ideal empty mind.

Now that we are deeply into the make-up of your pre-shot routine you may be wondering why we are not suggesting you should seek to emulate Jack Nicklaus, unarguably the greatest of them all, and visualize yourself hitting a good shot. We do not suggest this because we do not recommend it.

For most normal people it is too mentally demanding

to try to visualize a good shot. When you become good at golf you do have a mental *picture* in your mind, but this is not a visual picture. It is something you will find difficult to describe. It is more a half-verbal, half-mental knowledge of what the shot is going to be like.

Visualization is nowhere near as important as many people would have us believe. Like positive thinking, it sounds good – and skilfully deployed can be effective. But in inept or inexperienced hands the damage outweighs the potential. So think carefully before you decide to visualize each shot. Do not ask whether you can imagine the sight of a nice draw going high into the air and landing neatly on the green with just the right amount of backspin to tempt it back into the hole. Rather ask yourself if you can really visualize a shot you have probably never ever played.

Most of us have difficulty visualizing anything clearly. Often you will find that when you do try to visualize something like the perfect draw you will really be seeing a mental picture of a hook (with which we are all more familiar). And it will not be easy to get that image of a hooked shot out of your head.

If you are confident that you really can visualize what you intend and you want to make it part of your pre-shot routine, then go ahead and do it. Jack Nicklaus always runs a personal Hollywood spectacular through his mental moviedrome before every shot, even in practice. He opens with a picture of the ball nestling in its intended final resting place, then he cuts to a panorama of it getting there, and then the screen fades into the final scene which shows him making the type of swing required to transform his earlier visions into a reality. While such visualizing works for him, and even though he has often said he believes 'a few moments of movie-making might work some small miracles' for handicap golfers, Jack Nicklaus has always cautioned that the movie must show a perfect shot. 'We don't want any horror films of shots flying into sand or water or out of bounds,' he warns.

Looking at this movie-making business from the standpoints of the single-figure handicap of a Masters or the low-twenties of a Burns, we think Nicklaus is a true star. And on stage, screen and golf course there have been very few of these true greats.

We say it again – if you think your golf will benefit from visualizing success the Nicklaus way, then in his kind of language: 'Go for it!' If, like us, you are mortal then you are well advised to keep your visualizing away from the course and restrict it to a spot of 'home movies' – something you can see yourself working on as you relax at home before your next game. We will have more to say about this in Chapter 6.

The last item in your pre-shot routine is the Thought for the Day. Everything else in your preparations for the shot will be constant; the one variable is your Thought for the Day. As well as serving its main purpose of putting the mind into an all-but empty state, it also will serve to add variety to your pre-shot routine and to keep it fresh.

One of the potential problems with a pre-shot routine is that it can become too automatic, too natural a part of your game. So long as your routine is something you practise consciously it will serve to block out other thoughts; but once it just happens for you (which is the ideal we seek) there is the danger that undesirable thoughts will creep in. So the good thing about a Thought for the Day at the end of the pre-shot routine is that it is not an automatic thought, it changes round by round. You have to think about it. This solves two of your problems. The pre-shot routine has provided the rock to which you cling – something that is solid and consistent and unchanging, something that is always there to prevent random thoughts bouncing around in your head. And the Thought for the Day, coming at the end of the pre-shot routine, will maintain its freshness. And if it is fresh it will be effective.

Like your swing, your pre-shot routine is yours alone. Each one is unique. You can be as inventive as you like and you can make it as much fun as you like. The more fun you may make it then the more distinctive and effective it will be for you, and the more you will remember to go through it before every shot. The more you enjoy doing it, the more confident will be your swing and the more flowing your strike.

If you think you do not need a Thought for the Day – the kind of golfers who believe they can go to the movies with Jack Nicklaus may well forego such basic thoughts – you may care to finish off your pre-shot routine in the way many touring pros prefix their swing. They recite a single two-syllable word. The most-used is 'Tempo'. Mouthing it normally, though mainly silently, they will recite 'Tem . . .' on the upswing and '. . . po' as they come down on the ball. This, they claim, helps them achieve a smooth, relaxed swing.

Of course you now know why this ritual works; it helps them perform their natural swing without the normal smoothness being roughened and the relaxed flow being tensed-up through the incursion of intrusive thoughts or distractions. Even if those who adopt the practice do not realize why it works, they are in fact doing exactly what we recommend.

FIVE

═══════

AIM WITHOUT AIMING

I shut my eyes in order to see

Paul Gaugin

MILLIONS OF GOLFERS throughout the world would be playing better golf today, and would be far less concerned with their troublesome swings, if the importance of correct aiming had not been emphasized so strongly in their very first lesson. Most club professionals and golf teachers teach aiming as a necessary fundamental of the game; in this they are wrong. But as a result of their misconceptions the performance of millions of golfers will for ever be blighted.

Few would argue that there are three essential fundamentals – the grip, the stance and the swing. And the greatest of these is the swing. It is the most important because it encompasses all the other requirements for playing a good game of golf. If the swing is sweet and smooth and played in the right direction then the ball will, perforce, pursue an ideal path. The grip and the stance are necessary accoutrements of the swing; if the club is not held properly the ball will not be struck correctly. If the stance is not right and is not aligned with a perfect line of flight the strike will be off-target. The swing *is* golf.

But every golfer is taught from the beginning to think more about the *where* of his shot than the *how*. This is not

64

only true in golf. In the case of most sporting skills the one thing that always has been regarded as absolutely vital, both in the learning and in the performance, has been what is somewhat ponderously termed 'knowledge of results.'

The implication is that you cannot learn the skill of hitting a golf ball in the required direction unless you are able to see where it is going; you need to see what the ball does the moment you strike it. In the patois of the modern marketplace you require 'visual feedback'. The danger of misappropriating this technical terminology for sporting purposes is that it is understood literally – and, in its literal sense, visual feedback is a process in which the knowledge of results modifies the actions producing the result. In reality, visual feedback is the worst enemy of the golf learner and continues to plague most club players – and many professionals – for the rest of their playing days.

It is the insatiable appetite for a visual appraisal of the shot that leads golfers of all handicaps to lift their heads, many of them even before the club has struck the ball. We all think we don't do it, but we all do. Even Ballesteros once famously looked up in the Ryder Cup, topped his ball – and saw it go into the water.

Once lesser golfers have developed this headline fault it is enormously difficult to correct; players spend many unproductive years praying (and paying) for relief from this gnawing affliction. Not unnaturally, they seek a way of preventing their heads from rising on every strike. Unfortunately, in so doing they are seeking to remedy the effect rather than the cause.

The initial cause is the golf coach. Golfers are taught from the beginning to see their aim as the most crucial factor in their game. The pro will have admonished his novice golfers to take great care with their aim, warning them that every shot off line means an extra stroke on the card.

As a result the pupil develops the habit of looking up to see the result of his stroke – whatever the pro says about the importance of keeping the head still never seems to be more important than discovering where the ball has flown. In fact, you cannot keep your head perfectly still, because it comes up naturally when you sweep the club round and over the left shoulder at the end of the swing. But if it comes up before then, to satisfy the need to know where the ball has gone, it cements a lasting relationship between golfer and coach as pupil regularly returns to tutor in search of a cure.

Of course, golf teachers do not consciously encourage their pupils to raise their eyes to the trajectory of the shot. But by emphasising the importance of aiming they encourage players to monitor their aim and the natural way of doing this is to try to see where the ball has gone.

In fact, the golfer should have no need to make a visual check to discover where the ball has gone and what it did on its way there. Kinesthetic feedback – the sense of our own bodily position, weight, muscle tension and movement – allows us to judge whether or not a stroke was a good one. Did it have a rhythm? Did it *feel* smooth? Did it *sound* right? These things we know without having to look up to see where the ball has gone.

Research at the University of Trondheim in Norway in the mid-90s, led by Dr Rolf Ingvaldsen and Professor John Whiting, established new frontiers by proving this point – although the subjects were pistol shooters rather than golfers, the results confirmed that a visual knowledge of results is not important in developing a skill.

The researchers took two groups of unpractised pistol shooters and, over a period of time, taught them how to shoot. One group shot at targets throughout the experiment and always saw where their shots went. They had knowledge of results. Initially, the other group also shot at targets and saw the results; but then this second group was asked to fire into black holes so that they were unable to see the results of their shots. Later, this same group reverted to firing at targets and again saw the results.

When the results were analysed it was found that the two groups had achieved the same improvement in performance. Those who had their target practice interrupted by a lengthy spell of shooting into blackness were just as accurate as those who had continuously seen the targets. This finding went against all previous research which had suggested that it was essential to know where the shot had struck the target, where the ball was, where the serve had landed on the tennis court, whether the boast was up on the squash court.

When the researchers asked why this should be they concluded that the common underpinning of all skills is the co-ordinative structure – the ability to move the correct muscles, in the correct order, at the correct time. But the development of a co-ordinative structure is not dependent upon our knowing the results of our efforts.

More than any other skill, the golf swing relies on a sound co-ordinative structure. We have shown that the quest for a knowledge of results when striking the golf ball inevitably leads to a degradation of the co-ordination – the head comes up, or we thrash at the ball, or we make one of the many other imperfect movements that degrade our swing. If golfers were able to bring themselves to forget the result, to concentrate only on the intrinsic feedback available to them, instead of striving for accuracy, they would reach their targets more often.

Obviously the direction of the shot has to be factored into the equation at some stage, but this should not be until the swing and its attendant fundamentals have been developed properly. We do not believe that golf coaches can be encouraged ('educated' is a better, though perhaps rather unkind, verb) to teach their pupils that it is relatively unimportant to aim. We know how hard it is to teach an old guru new tricks. But we do insist that the only way to teach any new golfer how to realize his potential is to leave the Articles of Aiming hanging on a locker-room peg until the fundamentals (which include a proper line-up in the stance) have been mastered. Then the pupil golfer should be made to hit literally hundreds and hundreds of balls without aiming – until his co-ordinative structure has developed to the point at which he hits all his shots cleanly and smoothly.

Only when he has reached this stage should he worry about hitting a target. He will find that he soon gets the hang of lining up to the flag, and will be far more effective in hitting his target because he will have a better, a smoother, swing.

The golfer's ego, his inner drive to hit the target, interferes with his rhythm and makes his swing, and the resulting shot, far less efficient. Take away the motive to land the ball in a certain place and he will become better at executing the movement. His co-ordination improves and he develops more fluency, more rhythm, more speed perhaps, more strength, better power, better timing.

A good example of what we are talking about is provided by the different ways golfers react to a partner's good shot. Say your partner has hit a 6-iron within eight feet of the flag. You may not have thought about it this way before, but you now have a variety of options. You could be negative and tell yourself, 'Oh hell, that was too good – I can't match that.' Not the right approach, you will agree. Alternatively, you might resolve to be positive and say to yourself, 'Right, I'm going to put mine straight down the hole.' Not a good reaction, either, because most golfers never get a 6-iron approach shot to go directly into the hole.

What you should do is to tell yourself that you are going to get your ball *inside* your partner's ball. He is standing eight feet from the hole, so you are now setting yourself a target that is not $4^1/4$ inches in diameter (which

68

is the size of the hole) but a target that is 16 feet in diameter – or an area more than 2000 times the size! This way you have a much better chance of hitting your target. Even if you do not get inside your partner, even if you stop 10 feet from the flag, you have missed your target by only two feet. If you were aiming for the hole 10 feet is miles away. If you go for the bigger target you will play your shot with greater confidence and you will be more easily satisfied.

Jesper Parnevik, the Swede whose father is a stand-up comedian and who is not without his own idiosyncrasies, once drove to the wrong city for a tournament in his homeland, according to Jan Blomqvist, mentor of most Swedish professionals, who describes Parnevik as 'something of a space commander.' Certainly he desperately needed guidance from mission control when he was trying to land on the final green of the 1994 Open at Turnberry. His 302-yard drive had left him with a 130-yard approach to the green. He claimed later that he had not looked at the leaderboard and assumed he needed a birdie, or at least this was the reason he gave for deciding to go for the pin. He hit his sand wedge too boldly and landed in the grassy swale on the left of the green. This cost him a chip and two putts and gave him a bogie. If he had played an easy wedge to the middle of the green he would have left himself two putts for par and a play-off for the championship with Nick Price.

Laura Davies, perhaps not the most widely recognized, but certainly the most successful and most unaffected, of British sportswomen has won more than a million dollars and became world No. 1 without ever having a golf lesson. If she was like most of her contemporaries she would have her coach crouching behind her on the practice ground. But Laura Davies plays the game she enjoys playing the way she enjoys playing it. Sam Snead says: 'She plays the way I teach!' She can out-drive most of the professionals on the men's tours: a 300-yard drive is not unusual for her and she achieves it with the appearance of almost effortless nonchalance. Her marathon drives and her quiet confidence that she can comfortably reach every 470-yard par-4 with a driver and 3-iron are the products of practice.

Unwittingly, Laura Davies is the perfect embodiment of all the principles we propose. Her play is instinctive, guided by feel rather than sight. Her practice (not often and not for long) is for touch rather than technique. On the driving range she does not aim; as she puts it:

> All I want to do when I'm out practising is to loosen up a bit. Just think what'd happen if I tried to hit every ball straight and then found I was slicing them, or hooking, or whatever. It would only make me start to worry about it when I got out on the course.

There are all sorts of bonuses for the golfer who puts his game together in the right sequence, and leaves the aiming until he goes out on the course with a well-developed and robust co-ordinative structure. It will not take him long to adjust to the demands of getting the ball onto the green, of coping with the whims of the weather, or anything else. He will adapt confidently to shooting at his target, while his aim-orientated partners are still struggling to find a naturally smooth swing pattern.

The practice swing is a pre-shot routine feature of nearly all touring pros. It is something that your teaching pro will probably have sought to instil into your game plan. But like all harmless-looking things, it can be disastrous. Even if you have never done it yourself, you must have seen someone execute a copybook practice swing and then fall apart when they come to hit the ball. This contrast between practice perfection and disaster at the moment of truth can easily cast its blight over the remaining holes. The golfer needs to understand that when he executes his perfect practice swing he is not searching for a knowledge of where his ball would have gone. What is happening to him is that his co-ordinative structure is functioning beautifully and is endowing him with a delightfully smooth and rhythmic swing.

The practice swing is a false prophet. Beware these rehearsals unless you possess that unusual talent of being able to cut yourself off completely from any need to know where your ball ends up when you come to hit it down the fairway.

Instead of worrying about a practice swing which is quite likely to go wrong when it is repeated with a ball at the end of it, give some thought to the times you have seen golfers become so enraged and upset at the ball flying out of bounds that they have thrown down another ball and swung at it without giving a thought to the manner of the strike or the required direction. Most likely it will have gone 200 yards or so down the middle of the fairway.

Since Japan and the United States have grown to have so many things in common, it is not altogether surprising that these two countries should have the largest *per capita* golfing populations in the world. More than twelve million Japanese play golf, which is ten per cent of the population, as is the 25 million who play in America. Great Britain has three million golfers. What is so astonishing about the growing golf population of Japan is that there is no room in the country's 2,000 golf clubs for ten out of every twelve Japanese golfers. And most of those who do get onto a course have to travel for more than two hours to keep a tee time they booked at least two weeks, and more likely three months, ahead.

Those who get out to play will pay nearly £200 for green fee, caddie and something to eat. Each year they will pay about £1,000 for the latest in clothing, clubs and balls. Whether the existence of twelve million *kichigai* in Japan caused the country to become the world's largest manufacturer of golf equipment or vice versa is as perplexing a question as the chicken and the egg.

It is something more than keeping up with the Ozaki's and the Okamoto's that induces twelve million people to spend huge amounts of money on the latest fashion and the best clubs . . . and then go off to one of 5,000 golf ranges to hit balls nowhere. Perhaps the enthusiasm of the Japanese for golf without holes is due to the fact that they get a more deep-seated satisfaction, an inner glow of achievement, a contentment that is denied golfers in the West for whom the game is a conflict of emotions. The Western golfer ruins his swing because he thinks only about his aim; he misses his target because he's too confused about rebuilding his swing. The Japanese driver on the range constructs an ideal natural golf swing because he requires no external, visual feedback. His satisfaction comes from the feel of hitting balls in a multi-storey, city-centre driving range. These 'birdcages' are filled 24 hours a day, with perhaps 200 golfers paying £10 a visit (generally four times a week for beginners, seven times a month for the more experienced).

America is the holiday Mecca of Japanese golfers. In their tens of thousands, they hop across the Pacific to the Hawaiian islands and then on to California. In one year in the late 80s 41 per cent of the condominiums sold on Waikiki Beach were bought by Japanese. To follow a group of holidaying Japanese golfers is at once frustrating and fascinating. Those who are fortunate enough to play on Japanese courses (probably no more than a dozen times a year) are used to spending hardly less than six hours a round, usually with a break for lunch at the turn. Golf in Japan is too sacred an institution to bastardize with business; such talk is reserved for after the game in the communal bath or over drinks. At home or abroad, Japanese golf is something of a ritual which cannot be hurried.

Away from the birdcage, most golf for the Japanese is

on television. When they get onto a course they mimic the professionals on TV. They studiously line-up on the tee. They agonize over all their fairway lies, they pace about considering the hazards, they check the wind, whether it's there or not, by tossing tiny blades of grass into the air – and ignoring them as they fall back to earth. Always they mark their balls on the green after every putt. There are no gimmes, always they putt out. They do not mind playing slowly, nor do they mind waiting patiently for the slow group ahead of them.

What you see when you wait behind a Japanese group is what is obvious. What is not apparent is what lies beneath the surface of their game. Despite having little experience (if any) of playing on a course, they suffer from surprisingly few blatant mis-hits. They appear to waste time weighing up every conceivable hazard on the shot ahead, and yet they are forced to make very few bunker shots. And Japanese balls significantly lack the Western fascination with water.

Captivated by the apparent incongruity of non-golf course golfers comporting themselves – and keeping the ball in-bounds – with professional propriety, John Burns was lured into an unwitting *faux pas* when he waited behind a Japanese group on a short par-3 at the Tournament Players Course at Las Colinas in Dallas. After marking their balls, the four waved the Burns' party to play up, which it did – to the accompaniment of a mixture of (understandable) applause and (unintelligible) congratulation on every drive and every putt. Burns courteously thanked the visitors for being allowed through and led off to the next tee.

It was some time later that he discovered that the (thankfully) unintelligible utterances of the waiting Japanese on the rim of the green that punctuated his party's putting might have been more condemnatory than laudatory. Apparently they had hoped to watch the natives drive to the green and then to join in a communal putting feast – rather than see the locals putt out, pick up and pop off! Any golfers other than Japanese would have been disconcerted to have a group behind land balls on the green before they had played out their own.

The Japanese, most of whom have learned their golf in the same way as Laura Davies (by copying what they have seen on television), have an inherent feel for the game, as she has and as most of us do not. Davies says that when she wants to play a spin shot or finesse the ball she *thinks* the shot she wants to play as she addresses the ball. She says the ball goes where she had intended because something 'happens ' to her swing. In fact she gets it right because she is a natural golfer – she plays by feel. She is never put off by what is happening around her, she is immersed in her own game without being detached from the real world.

Many golfers who feel the need for visual feedback of the results of their shots also are easily distracted by what is going on around them. Putting can be a particular agony not only because it is the moment of truth but also because it is always witnessed by an audience of at least one playing partner and often three. Until you reach the green your companions will have had only a distant view of where your ball ended up. Now you will be conscious that they can see the line to the hole just as easily as you can.

As they stand and watch they may have more time than you to muse upon the ideal putting philosophy set out by Bobby Locke, arguably the game's best-ever putter. 'Every putt you will ever have in your entire life, on any course, in any country, of any length – is dead straight,' he said. Then he would make a concession to any concerns about the length and the lie of the grass, about the slope of the green and the break of the ball. 'All you can do, time and time again, is to hit it dead straight. But not necessarily, of course, straight at the hole!'

More than thirty years before the researchers in Trondheim had pistol shooters fire into a black hole, the colourful South African, who won four Open Championships and had fifteen holes-in-one, compared a putt on the green with firing a bullet from a rifle. In a high wind a bullet will describe a slightly curved line. The marksman will adjust his sights, aim straight at the bull – and hit it.

The Norwegian shooters who had first shot at targets and then into darkness probably still retained a mental image of the target. Richard Masters conducted a research project at the University of York, in conjunction with the work at Trondheim, in order to test whether withholding a knowledge of results from learner golfers affects the development of their co-ordinative structure. Like the shooters, the golf learners were asked to putt into darkness. The object of the exercise was to compare the development of co-ordination in those learner putters hitting putts only into darkness and those aiming at a real hole. It also provided an opportunity for looking at specific changes in jerk and stiffness as the skill got better. It need hardly be said that jerk and stiffness are two factors of vital importance in all putting.

Jerk was assessed by attaching an instrument which measured accelerations in all three dimensions to the back of the putter. As the player brought his putter back and then swung it forward towards the ball the researchers received a readout from the accelerometer on the rate of change in the acceleration of the club. That is, how jerky it was. Early on in the experiment the typical learner was highly jerky, but as he became more expert and his co-ordinative structure developed his jerk decreased. Most importantly, it was found that those who were putting into blackness became less jerky more quickly. This proved that they were developing their co-ordinative structure more rapidly than those who could see where they were aiming and were seeking to reach a target. In simple terms, not being aware of the result of the putt led to an ability to strike the ball more smoothly.

Stiffness in the putting action was also measured, following earlier research that had shown a relationship between the stiffness of the body in executing a movement and the degree of expertise of the performer. In the earlier work subjects were asked to draw a large treble clef (the musical sign indicating the position of G above middle C on the second line of the staff). When they came to the end of the clef, to the leftward hook at the bottom of the vertical, the flow of the arm was upset by a tug on a line attached to the wrist. The researchers discovered that the more expert the subject had become in drawing the clef as a result of practice, the more disturbed the drawing became. In other words, as expertise developed so the hand and arm controlling the pencil became less stiff.

Wondering if this would be the case with golf putting, the York researchers calculated the stiffness of the putting movement by arranging for an extraneous force (a blast of air) to propel the clubhead forwards immediately before the strike. The learner putters were comparatively stiff in their movements. When the blast of air struck their putters their stiffness acted as a brake and limited the impetus that was added to the strike. But when the air hit the clubs of the more accomplished putters who had become more relaxed through practice the ball was propelled much farther.

Between them, these research projects revealed conclusively that shooting and putting into darkness helped to develop a good co-ordinative structure. The subjects who had practised 'blind' in this way acquired additional fluency and gained a distinct advantage over those who had the questionable advantage of seeing what they were aiming at. When the first group of subjects were allowed to see their targets, they had a smoother, more rhythmic movement which helped them to achieve their objective.

There can be no argument (though, of course, there will be) that it is quite unnecessary to aim when you are practising. We realize that on the course there is an emphasis on where the ball has gone. Logically this has to be so if the purpose of the game is to propel (quite artificially) a ball from one point towards, and eventually into, a small hole several hundred yards distant, while negotiating a series of hazards. But if you have done as we suggest and evolved your own pre-shot routine, incorporating your stance and (essentially) your line-up, we repeat that you can forget about aiming. We do not say that you can simply dismiss the rites of aiming; we mean that you need never have to think about it again. That you will find aiming is something that happens naturally as you move through your routine preparing to address the ball.

It does not follow that because touring professionals look down at their ball and then up towards the target and repeat the process a number of times, that this process must be an integral, or even an important, part of every golfer's routine. Most people perform the ritual with the same degree of conviction as an American hoping you will have a nice day or a Briton enquiring after your health. Standing side-on to the target, it is impossible to judge the line with even the slightest degree of accuracy by swivelling the head backwards and forwards through a 90-degree arc.

Having forgotten about the aim, you have no urgent need to see the ball flying off towards the target, you can rely on your inner feedback, the sensations you feel as you strike the ball. Any thoughts you might have entertained remotely related to the direction of the shot will have been subsumed into a resolution along the lines of, 'I am going to make a smooth, clean stroke'. Your focus must be the sweep of the club, the feel of its impact. As you ask yourself whether this is the feel you wanted you will know whether the result was the shot you wanted.

It certainly will not be the shot you wanted if you spoiled it long before you reached the tee. Out on the practice range you might have begun to think too much about what you were doing. You would have these thoughts because you were consciously aiming. You would have been asking yourself: 'What do I have to do to get the ball to go over there?' You would have stopped concentrating on the need to make a clean strike, you would have messed about with your co-ordination and you would have misplaced any Thought for the Day. The driving range is a place for improving the swing and the strike – not for taking aim.

Most beginners (and many who began a long time ago) are interested only in where their ball goes, they do not have very much interest in the rhythm and the feel of the shot. They are not concerned to feel what Burt Lancaster called '. . . the tingle in your arms when you connect with the ball.' But that is what they should feel for, particularly when they are hitting practice balls. They should forget their concern for how hard the ball was struck and where it has gone. There is a good way to do this.

When you are hitting balls on the range (and you can carry this onto the course) do not look to see where your ball goes, instead award yourself a rating for each strike. Score your shots from one to ten. You would award yourself a one for a poor strike, not a clean hit, and a maximum ten for the perfect strike, the shot hit most cleanly that sounds the sweetest. After some time you will find yourself regularly scoring in the eights and nines and tens. Your rhythm and timing will be settling in and you will be warmed up to your swing.

You should begin with a favourite club, and when you are scoring those eights and nines and tens it is time to change clubs. If you are not getting top scores after a while you must make a decision: whether to change clubs or persevere. Changing clubs may be defeatist, but hanging on to the same one may compound whatever has become the problem. You will have to decide this for yourself, but if the scores do not get better – and providing they do not get worse either – try to persevere a little longer. If you do decide to change clubs and you have not got an easier club than the one you've been scoring low with, it's better to go home and start again another day.

Even if you get to enjoy scoring your strikes and start to notch up some good scores, it may still be very difficult to break that habit of looking up to see where the ball goes. It might help if you count to three before you look for the ball. Strike – one – two – three, and by now the ball will be well on its way, but it will not have landed and there will be plenty of time for you to follow it and see where it comes to rest. Do not think of this ruse as anything but what it is. It is another compromise. Keeping your head down as you count up to three will help you become less uptight and irritated about the way things are going. And you will still have the opportunity to check that the ball is going in the right direction.

Even if you make a conscious effort not to look, force of habit will inevitably triumph and you will look. But if you can go out onto the practice range and hit (say) twenty chips and then twenty 8-irons and then twenty 3-irons without once looking up between hitting the ball and it landing, you will almost certainly find that you have three sets of balls in remarkably compact groups, probably better placed than you have ever got them before. Your body will have done that for you while you were not looking.

When you have summoned sufficient courage not to aim consciously out there on the course but to leave direction-finding to your pre-shot routine, you will discover good things happening to you. In the back of your mind hang on to the idea that you are not going to aim, you are just going to hit the ball sweetly. You will find that you will strike the ball clean off the drive. Try it on the first tee and you will hit it dead straight. To your amazement, although you have not aimed, your body will have seen to it for you and your ball will have split the fairway.

So you are now saying to yourself: 'Well, my body won't do that for me . . . The only way I've any chance of getting down the middle of the fairway is if I do it for myself.' Most people do not trust their own brain, they feel the need to have conscious control, to be able to direct what they are doing. What golfers need to learn is to be able to trust themselves. They must let things just happen, and allow the body to sort itself out.

If this is a difficult concept, pause for a moment in your reading and ask yourself if you have been telling yourself *how* to read these words. Of course you haven't. You just read them, quite naturally. The principle is the same when it come to punching that ball down the fairway.

The brain is an amazing mechanism. At this moment it is doing an extraordinary number of things for you. It is monitoring the atmosphere and keeping your body at the correct temperature. It is listening for and registering all the sounds around you, but although it is registering them it is not interfering by drawing them to your attention. It will not alert you to these noises unless you ask it to do so. Then it will tell you there is a dog barking or a bird singing or a baby crying.

Your brain is well capable of controlling events and deciding what it should tell you. Sitting as you are, your leg may have begun to go numb and you will be so absorbed in the secrets and mysteries of your golf game that you will not have noticed any discomfort. Your brain will see no reason to disturb you until the numbness reaches a level of 'pins and needles' or cramp – then your brain will tell you it is time to move. The brain knows that if it told you before it would have been interfering –

interrupting and distracting you from your concentration. If it had allowed all those outside noises of barking dogs and screaming babies to impinge on your senses your reading would not have been so effective because you would be distracted. So transfer this principle onto the fairway.

If your brain starts interfering when you are playing golf, as it must if you tell it such things as 'I've got to hit this one dead straight,' it will interfere with your swing. If you leave your mind to get on with it – as it has been getting on with letting you read this chapter – you will play golf better, just as you read better. Allowing your mind to distract you on the golf course is not very different to letting it distract you when you are having a quiet read. Perhaps you should not complain so much in future about the children making a noise; perhaps you would have more peace if you did not ask your brain what the kids were doing.

You must have experienced, without ever realizing it, something the psychologists call the Cocktail Party Phenomenon. It's phenomenally simple really. You are standing in one of several disparate and probably disorderly groups. You are focused on someone in your party speaking, you are listening intently to what he or she is saying. You are not registering or understanding what is being said in other parts of the room . . . until someone somewhere speaks your name. Immediately you look up and you are aware that your name has been spoken. All the time that you have been wrapped up in the conversation of your own group of revellers your brain has been going about its separate business of registering everything that has been going on around you. Suddenly it has registered something it realizes is important to you: your name being spoken. 'Hey – that's you,' it tells you.

The lesson to be drawn from the Cocktail Party Phenomenon is that our brains are taking care of things, whether or not we are aware of the fact. Unless, that is, we interfere by insisting that the consciously, analytical side of us knows best.

If you want to split the fairway you must make sure there are not a lot of thoughts going through your head. You must not be thinking about the right direction, you will just be doing what Ian Woosnam *once* said he did. 'I just stand there and hit the damn ball. People think too much about golf.'

SIX

===

In Confidence

They are able because they think they are able

Virgil

THE REASON Big Bill Taft, the 27th President of the United States, described golf as 'a game full of moments of self-abasement, with only a few moments of self-exaltation,' was that he had learned, in the not-dissimilar political game, the overriding importance of confidence. Like a temporary lease on the White House, confidence is hard won and easily lost. In sport as in politics (and each contains many of the worst elements of the other) it may take many years to acquire the necessary confidence, and it takes very few moments to lose it all.

Every golfer knows another who displays an awful swing but has great confidence. He usually wins. We all know that other kind of player, the one with a superb swing but no confidence. He usually loses. All golfers, to a greater or lesser degree, belong to one or other of these categories. What makes the best players better than the rest of us is their ability to marry a good swing with a supreme confidence.

In 1994 there was little to distinguish between the thirty-year-old Scot Colin Montgomerie and South African Ernie Els, his junior by six years. Both are long off the tee and fine putters. Both are confident. Both play their golf without the ministrations of technical

advisers. They came head-to-head twice in 1994 and
Els won the US Open and the World Match Play four
months later because, as Kipling might have said, he
kept his head while his challengers were losing theirs.
Seldom does his confidence diminish, even for a
moment. Like Els, Montgomerie possesses the professional's ability to shrug off the bad thoughts, but it
takes him longer than Els probably because he makes
more fuss about them.

It is not the innocence of youth that gives Els greater
control of his confidence; whatever jealously ageing
observers may think, the six years from 24 to 30 do not
mark the transition (either mentally or physically)
from youth to middle-age. What separates Els from
Montgomerie and so many others is his outwardly
laconic determination to think that only good can come
out of anything.

Hettie Els understands, as only a mother can, what it
is that drives her son. 'He always knew within himself
that he was capable of these big wins and wanted it so
much,' she says. 'Ernie's not doing it to make a great
living, he's doing it to achieve.'

Els taught a useful lesson (to himself and to us all) in
the Masters a couple of months before he won the US
Open. After a birdie on the short 12th he became carried
away in the dialogue he was having with himself. His
confidence was growing even stronger now that he was
5 under par, and as he prepared to drive the par-5 13th
he got to thinking what his life would be like when he
became Masters Champion.

The 13th at Augusta National, called Azalea, has a
right-angle dog-leg to the left and demands a precision
drive. Many tournaments have been won and lost on the
11th, 12th and 13th of Amen Corner. It was not surprising, in view of his conversation with himself, that Els
pulled his drive into the bushes. The reason he did not
go on to follow so many other major contenders into the

mediocrity of the middle ranks is that he was able to talk himself out of his predicament so quickly and so firmly. Later he said of that wayward drive that it could have changed a lot of things – 'But we'll have another shot at it next year.'

His attitude is not the most common in the world of the touring pro and is decidedly uncommon among the millions of golfing commoners. Few golfers have acquired the one skill that is more vital to their game than any physical attribute. Anyone can swing a club and hit a ball, only a few have learned never to say anything to themselves – either on or off the course – that might possibly undermine their confidence.

Everyone talks to themselves. Most of the time they turn down the sound and just mutter away without speaking. A lot of internal dialogue just happens. But every thought we think is something that we are telling to ourselves. If you think about putting down this book you are telling yourself to put down the book, if you are wondering whether to pour a drink when you come to the end of the page you are asking yourself whether you should. Many people are not even aware of the things they say to themsleves. Perhaps this is why they will say things to themselves that they would not dream of saying to their worst enemy. And because they do not realize what they are doing, certainly they do not appreciate (or fear) the impact their monologue has upon them.

Most golfers who have come close to a big win – the club championship as much as the Open – but have surrendered to the pressure, never come that close again. They may be heard of occasionally in the monthly medal or an obscure tournament, but only the exceptional get to have another chance at the big ones. Once a golfer has talked himself out of winning the biggest prize it is immensely difficult for him to talk himself back into believing he really can do it next time.

Whatever happened to Johnny Bulla, R.W. Horne,

S.S. Scott, John Fallon, Dave Thomas, Fred Bullock, Phil Rodgers, Lu Liang Huan, and Simon Owen who were all post-war runners-up in the Open? What of Clayton Heafner, Ed Oliver, John Schlee, Forrest Fezler, or Lou Graham who all got within striking distance in the US Open?

The most dangerously disconcerting thing about the whole of this confidence business is that you can tell yourself that you are confident – and still be not confident. There are two important ways to increase your confidence or – and perhaps this is even more important – to prevent you losing your confidence.

The first is that you must have the correct kind of monologue going on in your head. The other is that you must have goals at which to aim. Having the right kind of target for your ambition (whether it is short- or long-term, the next shot or the year-long medal) is a marvellous way of creating confidence – as we will show in the next chapter.

Confident golfers are usually winners and winners are usually confident golfers. Trite perhaps, but unquestionably true. The golfer who lacks self-confidence, who doubts his own ability, is the one who is most likely to rely on the wrong club to perform the task he is not sufficiently confident to leave to his more favoured club. The golfer who plays the shot he does not know best and with which he is not at his most comfortable is the golfer who is unsure of himself.

In the 1992 Open Championship at Muirfield John Cook turned a one-stroke lead into a one-stroke defeat. Nick Faldo had seemed to give away the championship with dropped shots on the 13th and 14th. But he told himself: 'I have to play the best four holes of my life.' But when Cook three-putted the 17th, thus missing a birdie, he failed to recover his confidence. Down the 18th he second-guessed himself, changing his mind when he was about to take out his 3-iron. As a result he missed the green with his 2-iron, bogeyed the hole, and Faldo won his third Open by one stroke. When it no longer mattered, Cook admitted (not least to himself): 'I gave away the championship.'

The club that is blamed by most golfers is the putter. If any golfer possesses more than one club of any designation, it is always the putters that proliferate. Confidence is the putter-maker's worst enemy. The annual sales of the simplest club in the bag are directly proportional to the lack of self-esteem of those who use them.

The golf green is the graveyard of all our hopes and dreams. The perfect wood, the unwavering fairway drive, the homing approach shot – all become less significant when the hole, or the game, or the championship hangs on the putt. Which is as it should be. The putt is that final, climactic act that crowns the player's achievement. It is golf's *coup de grâce*.

Also it is the game's most debilitating confidence-sapper. It affects the princes of the game as much as the paupers. Colin Montgomerie, whose game relies heavily on a putting skill which is variously described as being between 'brilliant' and 'outstanding', summarized the problem admirably. 'You can win tournaments when you are not playing well,' he said in 1993 at a time when he was No 1 in Europe. 'But you can't win if you are putting badly.'

It is some consolation, to the rest of us, if not to them, that perhaps the two most celebrated problem-putters of the modern era have been Tom Watson and Bernhard Langer. Watson prefers not to talk of the 'yips' and calls his occasional affliction the 'flinch'. As we might expect from someone with such impeccable, self-induced confidence, Watson has never sought a release in homeopathic-type remedies. Not for him the broom-handle putter nestling in chest or chin, or the cack-handed grip Langer produced to combat his twitch in the late-80s, or the Putting Performance System of Harrogate coach Bill Ferguson.

Admittedly, several players have turned, quite successfully, to the long-shafted putter. More have adopted the grip Langer uses when he crouches over his short putts – left hand below right, the shaft pressed against the left forearm. We are unsure how many, apart from Montgomerie at one time, have practised with the Putting Performance System. Special practice balls are used which are of the regular weight but only fractionally smaller than the regulation 4¼-inch (108mm) diameter hole. The object is to encourage the player to hit the ball on the up, in the hope that when he comes to the real thing the golfer will think he is hitting the ball into a hole as big as a bucket.

But although any golfer who has swopped over to a broom-handle or begun to cross hands in the Langer style would passionately disagree, those who change equipment and begin to achieve better results are misleading themselves. We deliberately say that they *achieve* better results, which is not the same thing as *playing* better. Because he is engaged in a rather confused internal monologue as he searches for a remedy for his putting blues, the golfer imagines he is seeking to replace a faulty instrument with one that will work better. When it does sink more putts than his other club he believes he has bought the answer. This is nonsense. He has had the answer inside him all the time. The putter does not put the ball in the hole – the golfer does that. And it is his mind that engineers the entire operation for him. If he has been failing, it is because his mind has been failing him.

Denis Durnian had his richest year on the European Tour in 1989 when his new broom-handle putter helped him collect £145,000. Beyond riches, though, was a place in the Ryder Cup which seemed the nearest thing to a certainty until he missed the cut in five successive outings. When he was asked what had happened to his long-handled putter, he explained what he had done after finishing 25 strokes off the lead in the Portuguese Open, the penultimate European Tour event that year: 'I smashed it against a wall and threw the head in the swimming pool and buried the shaft in the garden. I wanted to make sure it was never used again.'

When the golfer suffers the yips or the twitches or the flinches consciously he seeks a new tool, a new putter to do what the original has failed to do. Or at least this is what he tells himself he is looking for. In fact, though, what he is really yearning for is a club that *feels* better than the one that he mistakenly believes has been letting him down and keeping his balls up. He wants to feel more comfortable, both with the club and with himself. When he finds such a club, when he is contented with the new partnership, he will say to himself: 'Now I'm much more likely to get the ball in the hole.' The new club is not going to perform putting miracles for him, but as soon as the golfer accepts it as a new and trusty friend, the simple existence of this new piece of equipment improves his confidence. He has begun a better internal monologue. And if his first putts with the new implement or the new grip start to slip into the holes, whether by luck or good management, the player's new confidence is further reinforced.

Johnny Miller, who won the US Open at Oakmont in 1973 and the Open at Royal Birkdale three years later, says: 'The hardest putt in golf is the four-footer after the four-footer!' Top golfers, every other golfer's heroes, are no less prone to talking and putting themselves into trouble than the rest of us. Some of them, though by no means the majority, get out of their troubles because they know what their troubles are. Unhappily for most of them not only do they continue to listen to their own negative monologue (which, if you asked, they would swear was positive) but they compound their difficulties by listening to every bit of advice they can get from everyone else.

Tony Jacklin is different. His name may never have been engraved on the temple walls, yet if he had not lived the impossible dream of holding both the Open and the US Open titles at the same time (1969/70) European golf might not have soared to its present eminence: a peak upon which he capitalized almost twenty years later when, as non-playing captain, he led Europe to Ryder Cup wins at The Belfry in 1985 and Muirfield Village two years later to end a United States domination that had begun in 1959. Jacklin was having putting problems when he gave up tournament play in 1985. The same problems were still there when he tried to engineer a come-back seven years later. He tried the broom-handle but it gave him no feel. He admitted that he was not confident, and because of that his head was coming up because he needed to see the result. He had lost his imagination. 'I've become a "how-to" when I want to be a "how-many" golfer,' he said.

At least he understood his problems better than most. No-one can cure those problems but the player himself. And to heal yourself you must have a proper monologue going on inside your head. Instinctively you must know the difference between negative and positive thinking, and you must make your confidence a real confidence. You need the kind of confidence that a Laura Davies enjoys. The kind of confidence that allows her not to aim on the practice ground – and the kind of confidence that allows her to sink eagle putts with her 3-wood. For the record she did this in the ShopRite Classic at Somers Point, New Jersey, in 1992 when she hit a 3-iron over the green on the par-5 8th. The ball finished up in tall grass twelve feet behind the pin. She took her 3-wood and rolled the ball into the hole.

Because Laura Davis has never taken lessons herself she is unlikely ever to give them. But every time she steps onto a golf course, she gives encouragement through her example. Her approach shot at Somers Point was one to savour, but it flew over the green. Because she possesses the kind of confidence to which all golfers should aspire, there was no negative talk with her caddie or inside her head. Just the confidence to select a favourite club – and sink the putt. Where other top players might have thought they were talking positively when they promised themselves they could get out of the tall grass and perhaps make the putt for a birdie, Laura Davies went for the putt from the rough with a 3-wood and walked off with an eagle.

As Rod Laver, the great Australian whose left-handed top-spin backhand won him two tennis Grand Slams, so fluently says of the golf game in which he was once down to scratch:

> If your swing isn't consistent in both games you'll have good days when it is and bad days when it isn't. And when it isn't you'll lose your confidence. And if you don't have your confidence you might just as well be a plumber.

It is the way in which you conduct your internal monologue, how you go about talking inside yourself, that mainly influences your confidence. When you walk towards a golf ball there is no time to reconsider negative words spoken to yourself, the damage is done only moments later when you swing the club. For most golfers the counsel they give themselves is bad counsel. It is usually negative. This is probably because most golfers feel there is more to complain about in their game than there is to rejoice over. Often this is far from true. If Walter Hagen could win eleven majors without hitting more than half a dozen 'perfect' shots in any one round, it does seem that a large majority of golfers find too much fault with themselves.

Next time you come in from the course and you are reviewing the day with the assistance of a large Weller's and Vichy water, ask yourself not how many times out there you remember being nice to yourself but how many times you said rude things to yourself. If you've left your pocket calculator at home, make an impromptu abacus with your macadamia nuts: put them on the left for the nice things you told yourself and on the right for all the nasties. Then eat from the righthand pile, because there'll be a whole lot more of them.

Inappropriate self-criticism usually occurs after what the golfer perceives to be a bad shot; but where Laura Davies finished, off the green, is where most approach shots end up. Which is why most golfers approach their most decisive shots with the wrong feelings about themselves. It is not surprising that a good shot that lands off the green should invoke a plethora of negative reactions. But while it rouses the uninitiated to anger, it gives the wise an opportunity to pat themselves on the back.

Of course, you can berate yourself for a well-hit shot that goes through the green, and you can go on to tell yourself how difficult it is going to be even to get down in three from where you are, relishing the dire consequences of a fate that is not really half as bad as you have persuaded yourself it is. On the other hand you could talk sense to yourself, think like the top pros do at their best. Remember how you have been scoring your shots for the feel factor when you have been practising. Instead of seeing the missed green negatively as a bad shot, score it for how it felt – a nine or a ten: 'What a great shot, really fantastic.' Then go on to talk to yourself just as positively about getting the ball into the hole: 'I've got a real chance of a birdie here.'

Accepting that a mis-hit was a good shot is being positive, but not half as positive as talking sense to yourself about the next shot. 'Birdie' – and bigger birds if that is not wildly optimistic – is a positive word. Birdies always look forward, they draw with them a surge of confidence – and you might even get a birdie. If Laura Davies can get an eagle with a 3-wood, why not?

Of course we are surrounded by cynicism, not least in a modern golf world where it is sometimes difficult to see the good in the game for the dollar bills. Cynicism is a bad self-counsellor; we can get too wrapped up in seeing the worst in other people's games to be able to see any good in our own. We even get to thinking that the occasional good things that happen are due more to luck than good management. The best players have a different attitude – the really best players, that is.

The most memorable moment in any golf *aficionado*'s video museum is Tom Watson's chip onto the 17th at Pebble Beach on the last day of the 1982 US Open. He was tied for the lead with Jack Nicklaus as he drove the 218-yards straight par-3. His 2-iron shot went high, with just a hint of a hook, and it bounced between two greenside bunkers before settling off the green in the rough. As he was preparing to chip with his sand wedge, his caddie told him: 'Get it close.' Watson replied: 'I'm not going to get it close . . . I'm going to make it.' The ball landed softly on the green and ran straight into the hole. And Tom Watson, the most undemonstrative of sportsmen, launched into an unaccustomed dance routine around the green – a man who knew that at last he had become the United States Open Champion.

Jack Nicklaus may have come to think of that shot of Watson's as his own least favourite shot, but he had enjoyed a similarly providential reward for his own massive self-confidence on the very same hole when he won the first US Open to be played at Pebble Beach ten years earlier. On that final day he played a 1-iron into the wind blowing in from the Pacific across the green and down the fairway. The ball took one bounce, nudged the pin and settled six inches from the hole to await his birdie putt.

It is better for the golfer's confidence if he sees these

seemingly random strokes of good fortune not as 'luck' but as a good 'break.' It is all too easy to focus on one's own misfortunes, and thinking you are unlucky is about as negative as you can get. If you start to believe you are unlucky, or even that you do not get your fair share of good luck, you will almost certainly provoke an onslaught of bad luck and a deluge of bad shots.

Jack Nicklaus, whose skill and confidence are unparalleled in the golf game, was distracted (and might even have given way to thoughts of bad luck) when he shot his highest Open score of 83 in the first round at Royal St George's in 1981. He knew that one of his sons had been hurt in a car crash back home. By the time he went out the next day he had been told the injuries were only slight and he saved almost one shot per hole – this time he went round in 66.

Watson and Nicklaus would never see their shots on the 17th at Pebble Beach as lucky shots – they would count them for what they were: great shots. Accepting shots like these is just the same as accepting the bad ones. Whatever happens in golf is part of the fabric of the game. You must learn to talk yourself into accepting this. Accept all the things that happen, whether or not you are responsible for causing them. Accept the slice out of bounds, or the roll into the bunker when the ball hesitates before deciding whether to go in or stay topside, and accept the rub of the green.

And accept the conditions in which you are playing. Accept the heat of the sun (if you are playing anywhere but in Britain) and just as keenly accept the cold and the rain (if you are in the homeland of golf). If you are going to be upset by any kind of weather conditions it is better that you do not go out rather than that you should suffocate or dampen your confidence. If you do go out in bad conditions you can either complain to yourself about 'the bloody weather' or you can tell yourself you're going to have 'a bloody good time'.

Tom Kite, who respects the game as much as those in it respect him, credits Art Wall with some of the soundest advice that has helped his game plan.

> He said that I would make a certain number of birdies and pars and bogeys every year. It didn't matter one bit where they came. If they all came in one week, then it would matter. But not over a year. Now if you extend that principle over a lifetime, then somebody like me is going to win X tournaments and blow Y tournaments. Over a lifetime it doesn't matter where they come.

Laura Davies has her own way with words: 'You've just got to have fun,' she says. 'Otherwise golf would be too much like a real job.'

There is little doubt that when people begin enjoying themselves they become more efficient. Which probably explains why the Western world is riddled with over-bearingly incompetent bureaucrats. Lots of people who play good golf can be pretty overbearing, too. The Americans say we should not do something because we have to do it, we should do it because we want to do it. Which is all very well – until the want turns into an obsession which develops into a mania which spawns paranoia. Wanting something too much has turned both the men's Ryder Cup and the women's Solheim Cup into national confrontations – on both sides of the fairway ropes. And there is now a very real danger that these genuine showpieces of golf will involve an honourable pastime in the kind of crass conflicts that have overtaken most other major sports.

Pride has come before the fall of all those sports. National pride, town pride, personal pride. But no form of pride is synonymous with self-confidence. Being confident, respecting both yourself and your game, is not arrogance. Arrogance is physical; confidence resides in the mind. Of course, if you grub a ball along the ground and turn away calling yourself an ass (or any other apt euphemism) then you are more likely to play like a complete ass at the next hole. On the other hand, if you tell yourself that even the best players do it occasionally and concentrate on thinking yourself into your pre-shot routine for the next shot, then you are more likely to play yourself right back into your game.

Even the top professionals have problems with their emotions, particularly if they hit a couple of bad shots in a row. They begin to get angry with themselves and see their score falling apart. This is when they have to choose the words they speak to themselves with the same care they select their clubs and fashion their shots. Words can be more cutting than the wildest slice; they can be more satisfying than the sweetest birdie. It is useful to have in mind your own thesaurus, an anthology of antonyms for your game's disasters. Select some passwords, a number of back-on-the-tracks expressions. No-one else is going to hear them, so you can make them words or phrases that have special meanings for you, anything that you are confident will put you back in the right mode and mood: words that will trigger a positive monologue within yourself.

In the nicest way (he would have you believe) Richard Masters was once accused on the golf course of being petulant. He was so stung by the admonition that he could be irritable and impatient over ill-considered trifles that the word has stuck in his mind in capital letters. Whenever now he becomes (as he puts it) 'wound-up', he tells himself: 'Don't be petulant!' This immediately sparks a positive attitude within himself – because it makes him laugh.

The idea is to carry around with you a ready-made antidote to any degree of annoyance or frustration or anger. Knowing that you have these key words in your confidential armoury is one thing – going into your next round of golf saying to yourself: 'Right! Now I'm going to make a real effort to maintain a positive dialogue with myself,' will not succeed. It will not work because it's too ponderous. You do not talk like that and you are not going to have a useful dialogue going on in your head if you pepper it with pompous phrases.

Old habits die hard, and unless you have done your homework on yourself it will not be long before you are cursing yourself for your stupidity over another mangled shot. It is through force of habit that you must learn to counsel yourself into being a confident player. Practice is the only way. In the same way that your swing must come naturally and without external effort, so too must your inner confidence. And the best way to maintain your confidence is by positive dialogue. Bobby Jones and Ben Hogan and Jack Nicklaus – the three greatest – would not say the rude things about or to themselves that are commonplace among many of today's players. Even some of the top names are adept at calling themselves names – and not only in their private thoughts.

Generally it is life's losers who say the cruellest things about themselves. Golfers fall into this trap when they are not on a winning streak. And they are not on a winning streak because they have the wrong kind of words running through their minds. There are those who react by arranging a $500 hour-long consultation, or adopting a modified grip, a flatter swing plane, a stiffer arm or a more flexible upper leg. But there is nothing fundamentally wrong with any golfer below the neck. And the problem above the collar is so often self-induced.

Too many players at all levels expect to be able to decide when they win or, within a stroke or two, how many they will card. They cannot do this. Golfers can only go out there and play the course and wait for the day. And while they wait and play, the nicer the things they say to themselves the quicker that day will dawn.

Anyone who says he never says negative things to

himself is, in the language of the British political classes, being economical with the truth. The difference between the touring pros and the club golfer, between winners and losers, is that a lot of club golfers and a lot of losers let the negative things stay in their minds, which become cluttered with negative attitudes. The better pros and winners of all kinds may say something superficially negative to themselves after a bad drive or a missed putt, but they have the practised ability – or a natural facility – to replace it almost immediately. They drop it, forget it, and just carry on. They have learned how to accept. But there are many more struggling professionals, who hit as straight as anyone on the driving range, who would do well to learn this.

Positive thinking means never saying you will not do something. Never say to yourself that you will not put the ball into the bunker that yawns in your path. Instead, ask yourself if you can pop it right into the hole. When it comes to it, chances are you will not put it in the hole, you will miss the hole – but you will not have put it in the bunker. That is what self-counselling does for you – missing the hole is a small price to pay for not landing in the sandtrap.

If you have endured a long spell of telling yourself not to slice, while doing so nevertheless – try a change of tack. Don't tell yourself 'I'm not going to slice this', but rather say 'I'm going to draw it.' You may not draw it very often – but you won't often slice it, either!

There is a great deal of sound common sense in the teachings of the Zen Buddhists, the Japanese sect that seeks enlightenment through meditation and intuition rather than in traditional scripture. Much of it is too readily dismissed as mere mysticism. Good golfers play better golf intuitively when they have no conscious recollection of traditional learning. The 'childlikeness' that Suzuki says needs to be restored with long training in self-forgetfulness is the natural ability to think about something without knowing it. A child does not say to itself: 'I am going to walk across the room and pick a biscuit off that plate – but I must be careful not to knock the plate onto the floor.' The child wants a biscuit, so it rushes across the room and grabs one. But the adult will tell himself: 'That's a delicate plate. It must be rather precious. I must be careful not to knock it.' And just because he takes so much care to be careful he smashes the plate on the floor.

Older club golfers often speak in awe of how the youngest players are such amazing putters. They are reminded of how they were good putters, too, when they were young. The reason is that the youngsters do not walk up to the ball and tell themselves: 'I am now going to knock this ball into that hole.' They just do it. And they play the whole round with the same approach.

But their days are numbered. Like the innocence they might once have had, the 'childlike' ability that does so much for their golf is about to become forfeit to traditional coaching. The games they have modelled on their golfing heroes are to be fine-tuned by the club pro. With the best will in his world he will tell them: 'You must grip like this . . . Start to think about it.' And so they do, and they begin thinking about everything they do, and, inevitably, the thoughts become negative because they do not always hit good shots – and no-one has told them how they would hit more of their good shots by talking only positively to themselves. Introspective thought is seldom neutral. It is either positive or negative. So you might as well make it positive.

Yet the ultimate goal is not a mind devoid of negative thoughts or a mind that is force-fed with positive thoughts. Our ultimate remains The Empty Mind in which absolutely no thought goes on. The ideal of the empty mind is such a priceless goal that you should think often of that best shot in your last round or, if you can remember it, the best shot you ever played. You should try to recall the thougths that accompanied it, what was going on in your mind at that time. You will recall the shot but you will not remember the thoughts. Because your mind will have been empty. Probably not consciously emptied, but empty.

It is very difficult to encourage people to banish their internal monologue, to stop talking within themselves; really to stop thinking in words. But you will find that if you are able to replace your negative thoughts with positive ones, then after a time this will so improve your confidence that you will get to a state where you can go up to the ball with a much better chance of having an empty mind. When your mind is emptied of thoughts of mis-hits and all other problems it will begin to feel the sun and smell the roses. And you will be confident.

A positive dialogue is like the Thought for the Day – neither is the ultimate. They are a couple of building blocks upon which to erect your confidence. And when that confidence is complete it will open the door to an empty mind.

When we entered our caveat about visualization in Chapter 4 we conceded the possibility that you might gain some benefit from indulging in a restricted form of home movies, rather like the armchair practice Nick Faldo sometimes does. He sits at home and quietly plays through in his mind the best shots he believes he has ever played – from his Open win at St Andrews in 1990.

Visualization like this is only useful if you are good at it. But if this kind of thing is for you it might help you towards a positive internal monologue and enable you to respond better and more positively to your poor shots. Like Jack Nicklaus, Faldo is able to dream up his best shots. We suggest you do quite the opposite. Visualize yourself hitting a poor shot off the tee. See it go into the trees and get stuck behind a large beech. Picture yourself doing all the bad things – throwing down your club in anger and saying all those negative things to yourself.

Now switch the cassettes in your mind. See yourself remaining calm after the bad shot, talking positively to yourself. Walk up to the ball relaxed and don't thrash at it as you did in the first reel. This time take your favourite club and chip the ball sideways onto the fairway and follow it with a good third shot towards the green.

These are a couple of good movies to play in your mind at home, if you are into these things. They are one more way of looking at the good and the bad in golf and seeing only the prospect of good in the bad. We all have to make the best out of our lives and few of us have lives that are all good. Play the same kind of golf. Tell yourself the good things and banish the negatives.

Greg Norman always keeps handy some words of Franklin Delano Roosevelt. 'I would rather experience the ecstasy of victory and the pain of defeat than spend any time in the grey twilight of life,' said FDR. 'That's the way I want to play my golf,' says the Shark.

That's the way we should all do a lot of things.

SEVEN

====

GOAL KEEPERS

The man without a purpose is like a ship without a rudder

Thomas Carlyle

IF PIERRE DE COUBERTIN had invented the game of golf (which has held to its principles far better than the modern Olympics he did create) he might have observed that the important thing in golf is not so much winning but improving. The golfer's greatest goal never varies from the dawn in which he collects his first score-card to the twilight in which he puts in his final tally. No matter how age may have wearied him, nor how the years may have condemned his youthful swing to a *distance* memory, every golfer can go on striving to improve until he chips in on that final hole.

There is no greater joy than hearing the sweet sound of the strike as it cuts through the ball, of draws and fades that come true, of scores that come down. There is even more satisfaction to be found in the least discernible improvement in your game than in contradicting all probability with a miracle hole-in-one.

Why else but to advance their insatiable quest for improvement do top pros change swings that to the rest of us seem heaven-sent? These masters of the craft of golf – comforted by their caddies, agents, managers, golf coaches, exercise coaches, nutritionists, physios *et al* –

cannot see their peaks for their plateaus. They want to run golf's three-minute mile, to play Nick Faldo's perfect round of 52.

At once they are doing all that is right and all that is wrong for their game – they are setting themselves new goals. Without goals no golfer's game will flourish, but with the wrong goals it will waste away. Many of the top pros who have achieved all their goals allow their peak to broaden into a plateau of despair. They have discovered there is no better than best, yet still they suffer the urge to improve.

So they set themselves wrong goals. For the first time in what may have been an outstanding career they begin to seek unrealistic and unattainable goals. They become the martyrs of the world's fairways. They nurse fairytale dreams. They believe the gods will deliver them to a state that lies beyond their richest reality. They fail to see that they are no different to the rest of us – no-one is completely satisfied with the way he plays. Every winner is as anxious to improve his game as much as every loser.

Having goals in golf is vital whether your handicap is at the top or at the bottom of the scale. But they must be realistic goals; they must be achievable. Scrapping a swing and building a new one is not realistic – unless you are a Faldo, whose single-minded dedication to his game outstrips even that of Ben Hogan.

Many of the world's top players and just about every other golfer in the world has modelled some part (if not all) of his game on a hero from his early days. Nick Faldo is a role model *par excellence* – more for what he has been seen to do than for his highly individualistic methods of doing it. Anyone who lacks the single-minded devotion to his craft that Faldo embodies would be foolish to dismantle as delightful a swing as he displayed for his first ten years on tour. For his own unique reasons, Faldo worked with his coach David Leadbetter to construct a replacement swing: he did not believe it was standing up to the pressure, he thought it was not giving him the control he needed when he wanted to fade or to draw at will. Most of all it had not won any majors for him.

His stylish swing was no longer capable of achieving his goals. He no longer wanted to win what he called 'ordinary' tournaments. 'I want to win the majors,' he said at the time. 'And the first I want is the Open.'

Faldo's swings and his *persona* will become established as the game's greatest enigma. Before he became the proud possessor of a manufactured swing designed to be the ultimate, he had experienced what he thought were nightmares. In one he was struggling, and failing, to chip his ball into a large wine glass placed on the ground. He could not get the ball high enough – but other players around him did. In another 'nightmare' he was not able to take the club back because of an obstruction behind the clubhead.

After being two years in the making, the new swing did for Faldo what President Clinton claimed to have done for Haiti – turn the nightmare into a dream. In Faldo's case he really did dream that he would win the 1987 Open at Muirfield, the oldest golf club in the world and home of The Honourable Company of Edinburgh Golfers whose 'Thirteen Rules' were the game's first. That Open Championship was Faldo's first major. His new swing (or was it really the confidence the new swing was giving him?) quickly brought him more major successes – two more Open championships (at St Andrews in 1990 and Muirfield again in 1992) and back-to-back Masters titles (in 1989 and 1990). He had won five majors in a half-decade during which only Curtis Strange (US Open 1988 and 1989) and Payne Stewart (US PGA 1989 and US Open 1991) won more than one.

After a five-year honeymoon with his new swing, Faldo again began suffering from the vagaries of fortune. Sometimes it was his putting that caused the agony, at others it was his irons or his woods. No-one seemed to ask what might be the real cause of his changed form. Might it not have been that after so desperately wanting to win a major and collecting five in five years (and becoming the first British golfer to win the Open Championship three times since Henry Cotton in 1948) Nick Faldo was running out of goals?

Might it be that he was setting the wrong goals? Might it be that he won those five majors as a result of the confidence inspired by his new swing? Might it be that the novelty and the faith in a new swing had to wear off some time – and reality return? A swing that had taken 28 years of his life to become natural had been replaced by a one that did wonders for him for five years and then stopped delivering.

In the departments where it really matters, there is very little difference between the top pro and the Sunday morning golfer. The amateur does not have his own coach to help him set correct goals, the professional has his attendant guru who probably does not know what a good goal is. More golfers would play better golf if coaches taught their pupils how to set specific, constructive goals. But 'Who will teach the teachers?'

During the later part of the period when Leadbetter was inducing 'feel' into Faldo's reconstructed swing with the aid of assorted water-wings, medicine balls, fishing rods and rubber bands, on the other side of the world, in Australia, sports psychologist Jeff Bond was working with a 22-year-old tennis player called Pat Cash. Bond was testing his belief that athletes in general can achieve greater success if they focus on the method instead of the end product. In effect he was testing his theory that setting a series of subordinate goals is more effective than concentrating on the big prize. He was not discounting the supreme importance of striving towards the final goal, rather he was testing whether a blind

concentration on the end result alone made it more difficult to achieve the performance that was necessary to get
there.

Bond had developed his theory after seeing athletes
under stress at the Los Angeles Olympic Games in 1984.
'Highly-trained, finely-tuned athletes failed because
they could not handle the pressure,' he said. 'They
choked not because they weren't good enough but
simply because of the nature of the competition.'

Bond's principle of 'process versus outcome,' in
which the performer concentrates on the skills and the
final result becomes the logical culmination of a series
of intermediate goals, was to place Pat Cash in the
Wimbledon final of 1987 with a totally different set of
goals to Ivan Lendl. Lendl went out once again believing that his whole life depended on that match. Cash
had a set of goals to help him play top-quality tennis
in 'just another match'. He had been schooled to have
no goal beyond winning the point he was currently
playing. Twice in the match he did not know that he
had taken a point to win a game. When he won his final
volley, Cash paused in mid-court for a second: he had
been concentrating so hard on his goal of winning the
point that he did not immediately realize that he had
won Wimbledon.

Many golfers (unlike most other sportsmen) fail to set
themselves any goals. Many more golfers (like people in
other sports) give up the game because they do not
achieve their goals – not simply because they fail to
realize them, but because they are impossible. Some
professionals who have the good sense not to set unrealistic goals give up their games because they run out of
gettable goals.

Ian Baker-Finch, the gentleman Australian, was only
34 when he talked of 'walking away for ever' after
missing ten successive cuts on the US Tour in the latter
half of 1994 and then two more in Japan. 'If it continues

to happen too much longer,' he said, 'I'll just stop playing. I'm not doing it for the money. I just do it because I want to play as I know I can.'

Baker-Finch had realized his greatest goal only three years earlier when he won the Open at Royal Birkdale with such superb self-confidence. He had a 64 (6-under par) on the third day and in the final round he had five birdies in the first seven holes and went out in 29 – something no other 'champion golfer' has ever done. Partnered by his friend and Florida neighbour Mark O'Meara (who finished joint third, three strokes behind), Baker-Finch had a finishing round of 66 – and it took them only nine minutes short of four hours.

When the claret jug was in his hands he admitted the Open was the most special event in his life. 'Just to play in it is great. To do well is fantastic. To win it is a dream.' Then he offered two contradictory thoughts. Reflectively (perhaps remembering earlier Open disappointments in 1984 and 1990), he said: 'You start feeling a lot of emotions out there. But just because you fail, it doesn't make you a failure.' And then came what was to turn out to be an ominously prophetic thought: 'I am sure every winner of a major championship thinks it is going to be the first of many. But now I've got my hands on this jug, I don't care about anything else.'

Two years later Baker-Finch climbed on the bandwagon and tried unsuccessfully to rebuild his swing. The following year he was talking of giving up golf. 'There is a hell of a lot of pressure that builds up because you start doubting yourself so much,' he said. 'And your confidence level gets so low that you wonder whether you'll ever play well again.'

Ian Baker-Finch's problems were neither unusual nor unique. When he was 24 years old Björn Borg won his fifth successive Wimbledon singles title, beating the twenty-year-old John McEnroe in the championships' most exciting final. One year later he left the game

107

because there were no goals left and he entered an 'empty and monotonous' afterlife. Ivan Lendl was at the top of the tennis game for many more years because he had an attainable goal that he never achieved: he wanted to win Wimbledon. The moral of such stories is that many players of greater or lesser ability play on into ripe old age, not because they are fitter or better than those who retire but because they still have goals.

Setting goals in golf is as important as your stance, or your grip, or your swing. Goals are as important as the pre-shot routine, as rewarding as a Thought for the Day, as desirable as the ultimate empty mind. A goal can be long-term or it can be immediately attainable – to drop your handicap by a couple or a dozen strokes by the end of the month or the year, or to sense that every shot hit today is hit sweetly.

If you have never set yourself goals before you should beware of some pitfalls. Every goal you set yourself must be possible for you to achieve. It is no good having a goal that you know a better player might achieve, he will not be playing your game for you. Your partner may be capable of going round the course in less than 10-over par. You may never have bettered 20-over. If you set yourself a goal of single figures, not only will you be depressed when you do not finish the round in less than 10-over – you will be distraught when you go well over your regular 20 or so.

You must make your goals both interesting and challenging. It is obvious that if the goal is not interesting it will lose its attraction. If it is not challenging the joy in achievement will be ephemeral; tomorrow you will have lost interest. The goal must be a shot too far, a score marginally better than your average or your best, a perfect shot, not from the worst club in your bag, but from your second-best – then from your third-best and progressively down to your most difficult club. No worthwhile goal is ever the ultimate, it is just one more step on the right road.

If you go for the unattainable you will not feel yourself improving and you will become depressed, which is more than understandable if you go to all the trouble of thinking up goals and then you cannot see yourself getting any better. Either you will get depressed about yourself or angry that we got you into another fine mess. You should never allow yourself to become depressed with your game in general or your ability to achieve your goals in particular. Depressed golfers lose their motivation. And when you lose that inner drive you will not go out to practise and you will soon start making excuses about the weather being too cold or too hot even to go out to play.

When you have some interesting and challenging goals, make sure they are intelligible. Do not let them be vague. Do not aim to go round 'a few shots' better than last time or play 'a few more' holes in regulation. Be clear and concise. Afterwards – after the round, or after the week, the month, or however long the target period for achieving a particular goal – you are going to have to evaluate the benefits. Unless you started out with a precise goal there will be no standard by which to measure.

If your goal was to reduce your score by a specific number of shots or to par a certain number of holes you will have a yardstick for measuring if you attained it, or, if not, by how far you fell short. If you have only a vague ambition you can expect only an imprecise result. And that will make you more depressed than just missing the goal.

Missed goals in golf are not the life or death matters they have become in other fields of sporting conflict. If you have not achieved your goal by the target date then you may have to set another date. You may have to set yourself a stricter schedule to help you get there. If one or two rounds a week is not achieving the objective, perhaps you need to practise once or twice a week as well. If you do need to tighten your schedule, remember it must be strict. One or two rounds a week and one or two practice sessions are not either/or options. If you opt for twice a week then once is never enough.

You might have to look back on your fundamentals. You might even have to ask your club pro to have a look with you. After all, 'A Swiss watch doesn't know how to repair itself' – as Tony Penna once said after he had given Sam Snead a lesson. But remember the doctor and patient relationship: you want to know what is fundamentally wrong and what simple cure would right that wrong: you do not want the whole works.

Struggling to reach goals that are beyond your abilities is not only exceptionally demanding, if you genuinely struggle to reach them, it is also particularly damaging to your confidence. If you are never going to do anything that will belittle your belief in your own golfing abilities, never aim above yourself. When you go out with your regular golfing partner, who always beats you, it would be foolhardy to set a goal of beating him. The day may come when you will be able to beat him, but for now you need to set yourself some attainable goals. For example, in losing you might have achieved a lot. You might have played a lot of good shots. You might have carded what is a low score for you. You might have done any number of things that, had they been goals in themselves, would have ranked as successes. So if you build your entire game on a pyramid of achievable smaller goals you will gradually get closer to the main goal while maintaining your confidence in yourself.

But you must avoid setting yourself negative goals. For example, if you have not yet succeeded in following our injunction not to look for feedback every time you hit the ball and you are still topping the ball, you might decide to set yourself the goal of not topping the ball. That is much too negative. If you let yourself think about this goal when you are about to strike you are going to increase your chances of topping the ball until it becomes almost a certainty.

If you want to stop topping the ball, aim to do so by the end of your next two rounds; you need time for any goal to be achieved. If you want to make this your Thought for the Day by all means do so, but make it like all single thoughts before the strike: make it positive. 'I'm going to slide the blade between the grass and the ball' is positive. That is something you can feel – and a feedback for which you can be encouraged to look, because if you are watching the club slide between grass and ball you will not be thinking of executing a smart 'Eyes Left' in search of where the ball is going. How you hit the ball (which is what not topping it is all about) is critical in determining where it goes. So you will achieve another goal, another step towards putting together a better game – and a massive boost to your confidence. And the great thing about confidence is that it is cumulative. Being confident about one part of your game encourages confidence in other parts.

Greg Norman had as much confidence as he had charisma in his first decade as a professional. He peaked in 1986 when he had two wins on the US PGA Tour, was runner-up four times and had ten top-ten finishes out of nineteen starts. He led by one stroke going into the final day of the Masters Tournament and finished tied for second place with Tom Kite. He led by one again after three days of the US Open and finished in a tie for twelfth place. In July he crowned his season by becoming 'the champion golfer for the year' when he won the Open Championship at Turnberry. The next year he saw Larry Mize sink a 40-yard chip for the Masters title as he tied again for second place, this time with Seve Ballesteros. Two years on he put his drive into a bunker on Royal Troon's 452-yard 18th in the play-off of the Open. Mark Calcavecchia's 5-iron approach landed seven feet from the flag – and Norman had another major tie for second place, now with Wayne Grady. After that it took him nearly four years to come in from the cold, four years to set his goals in order. Four years to realize 'I made the dumb mistake of changing my swing and it's taken all this time to get back my natural style.'

He began to admit the damage those defeats in the majors had done to him. He began telling himself that he would never play great golf again if he allowed his mind to be strong on the negative side. 'But if it's strong on the positive side, then you're going to be around for a long time, no matter what people say or do to you,' he says. 'The whole crux of the deal is that you believe in yourself and you don't believe fate's against you and you don't believe in bad luck.'

Before the Open Championship at Royal St George's in 1993 Norman had begun thinking deeply about the mental approach to golf. He began to learn how to put himself in the right frame of mind to succeed. As he stepped off the 18th green on Sunday 18 July Gene Sarazen, who had been runner-up to Walter Hagen in the same place in 1928 (and who had won his own Open on the same dunes next-door to the north at Prince's in 1932) told Norman: 'That was the most awesome display of golf I've ever seen.' Also it was a classic example of successful goal-setting.

Since that glorious day proved he was not a one-major man, Greg Norman has often talked about getting into the right frame of mind to succeed, how he has begun to *want* things to happen. As he played the final round of the 1993 Open Norman recalled how the great basketball player Larry Bird had told him that once, with five seconds to go and his team losing by one point, he had *wanted* the ball. When he hit a 9-iron on the 9th two inches from the hole to take a one-stroke lead Norman remembered his friend. 'All the way in on the back nine I was reminding myself what Larry said. I really *wanted* that one-shot lead.'

Gene Sarazen's 'awesome' accolade could not have been more apt. Then 91 years old (and still ceremonially teeing-off the Masters) he brought to mind words written by Henry Longhurst in the 50s. Describing Sarazen as the simplest golfer he had ever seen, Longhurst wrote:

> He stood with both feet rooted to the ground, grasped the club firmly in both hands with a couple of inches of shaft showing at the top and hit the ball a tremendous, elementary thump. When I get fouled up in the mechanics of the game I can still produce a series of reasonable shots by forgetting the theories and imagining that I am Gene Sarazen.

Sarazen won the Open Championship once, the US Open twice, the US PGA Championship three times and his win in the second year of the Masters (1935), was to be the making of the tournament because of one stroke he played on the 500-yard 'Firethorn' 15th on the last day. Sarazen drove to the centre of the fairway, leaving himself a 220-yard approach shot to a green that stands protected by a lake across its entire face. Having scorned the spoon his caddie suggested, he took his 4-wood instead. At this moment he lay three strokes behind Craig Wood, the tournament leader in the clubhouse. When his ball went into the cup for an albatross he was tied for first place and went on to win the play-off the next day.

One of the biggest failings of amateur golfers – and of many touring professionals, too – is not setting correct goals. We said earlier in this chapter that many golfers do not set themselves goals; it would probably be more accurate to say that although most golfers do not deliberately set goals, they do still have goals of sorts. The problem with these 'goals' is that the players really do not realize they have them, they have not given any proper thought to them. Probably they are vague and unrealistic, almost certainly beyond their capacity, and they float in and out of their minds more or less at random.

There is no point in having an excellent swing or doing anything else on the golf course with great skill if it is not directed towards a specific end. The best golfers in the world more often than not fail to achieve their potential because they either lack proper goals or have set themselves the wrong goals.

There is very strong evidence that correct goals improve all sporting performance. Sceptics always will challenge the validity of any research, which is why the human race is so slow to develop; but while it may be sensible to challenge the conclusions of one research study, and it may even be legitimate to question the findings of a dozen separate studies, it would be foolish to deny the evidence of close to one hundred affirmative results. In 1981 Locke, Shaw, Saari and Latham (researching at the Universities of Maryland and Washington) claimed in the *Psychological Bulletin* that 99 out of 110 studies they had reviewed proved that specific, challenging goals produced better performances than easy, do-your-best type goals – and, to keep the record straight, better performances than no goals at all. A few sporting types had been included in these studies (such as swimmers and hockey players); the other subjects were key punchers, sales people, truck loaders, shipyard labourers, canning factory workers, pastry chefs, mail sorters, and assorted others.

A variety of research studies in the United States and Britain, particularly since the early 70s, have all concluded that specific, challenging but achievable goals lead to better performance and that they always create better motivation. This has been found to be as much the case with logging crews in Canada as with chess-players in Japan, as true of typists in England as of mathematicians in Massachusetts.

In one Canadian study 100 male college students were put through an endurance test in which they had to lift weights, one-armed, in time with a metronome beating 38 times a minute. One group was told 'Do your best'. Another group was told (casually) to do at least 40 repetitions; this was considered by researchers to be an obtainable goal. A third group was told that most males were well capable of 55 repetitions; this was not true, and a target of 55 repetitions was in fact very difficult.

Those set the almost unattainable goal had the best results, closely followed by the second group which had been set attainable goals. The do-your-best people were by far the worst. Yet in a strength test two minutes after completing their arm lifts, the second and third groups were found to be less strong than the students who merely had been trying to achieve their 'best'. The greater motivation created by their more challenging goals had led them to tire themselves more. Among the students who had been misled into thinking 55 lifts were within their capacity, the tests showed that relative strengths differed. Some had pushed themselves to exhaustion while others had given up when they realized they were not going to make the target of 55 lifts; for the latter the goal was too challenging. All of which confirms that goals are no good unless they are difficult – but that they have to be realistic and achievable.

If good goals are very, very good for you, bad goals are disastrous. You will escape disaster if you fail to achieve what is a good goal; but if you have a bad goal you will gain little if you attain it and you will do a lot of harm to you game – and probably yourself – if you fail to accomplish it.

It is common on professional tours to see a pro take a double-bogey as he comes towards the end of a tournament in which he is in contention. It is just as common as seeing the club golfer hit two out of bounds off the first tee. Both might have had goals, the pro wanting to win the tournament and the amateur having his sights set on going round in less than 10-over. Both players have their game ruined when they fall short of their goals; their confidence is shattered for the day, and the memory may remain to haunt their next excursions.

So every good and proper goal must leave scope for some flexibility. If you set yourself a do-or-die goal you will not be able rapidly to readjust when things go wrong. But adapting to new circumstances when the primary goal becomes out of reach can itself be fraught with greater hazards. When you set a goal – whether an immediate or a long-term one – you must leave yourself free to compromise and substitute an amended goal if the principal aim is no longer possible.

The art of good goal-setting is to set yourself a challenge that, with sustainable effort, you might extend yourself to achieve. When you get there, set another. If you fail, set another. But never, never tell yourself what the others are until you have need of them. The one-goal golfer is a positive, confident golfer. The player who consoles himself with prepared alternatives is without confidence and has little hope of reaching any real goal. You need to foster the ability to devise a fallback position. If your goal seems as if it is going to be lost by one bad shot, a rapidly revised goal will do wonders for your next shot. If you step up to the next ball still angry about dropped shots and a lost goal, you will probably ruin your pre-shot routine and the next shot will be at least as bad as the one that started what is fast becoming a rot. A quick new goal, new motivation, the same strong confidence – and your game will be saved. You may

116

even find that you end up achieving your original goal, the goal you thought had been put out of reach.

We are not suggesting it is easy to re-set goals out on the course, any more than we would suggest that golf is an easy game. But substituting new goals for old need not be a serious problem – unless you make it one. You have all the time in the world before you go out to play your next round of golf in which to set your primary goal. You have next to no time to come up with a lesser goal on the course when the first moves out of reach.

In the best traditions of vaudeville you should be encouraged to have well-prepared *ad libs* – at the back of your mind. If you take an unusually large number of shots on the first three holes – probably because you have set a goal of an unusually low score – you might come up with a well-prepared off-the-cuff suggestion to yourself to forget the score now and aim to get ten pars from the remaining fifteen holes. You might well shoot twelve pars and a very respectable total after all – because you have quickly come up with an alternative goal and not allowed your confidence to be upset by missing the original goal.

It is not just having correct goals that matters; how you get there is also important. Goals can be used to bring out the best in you but they can also bring out the worst. If you are aiming to come in in less than 10-over par and you have a disastrous eight on the first hole you might think that you have cause to be angry with yourself, to forget the day's goal and have a thoroughly miserable day. On the other hand, you could concentrate on averaging your score. A six on the next hole would bring your average down from eight to seven; even a seven would reduce the eight to seven and a half for the two holes. This will take the pressure off. Setting a new goal of getting par on every hole would put extra pressure on. On the downside, of course, if you shoot another eight on the second hole – start *ad libbing* to yourself again. Change from averaging scores to scoring your shots for sweetness and feel. When the challenge gets too hard remember to give yourself confidence wherever you can find it.

But you will never feel real confidence if you make yourself a gift of your goals. We have a formula for confidence: confidence is the result of positive thoughts added to frequent experiences of being successful. So it follows that if a history of successful experiences (achieved goals) equals confidence, then achievable goals produce a history of successful experiences. And specific goals lead to a better performance than general goals. Do Your Best may be all right for cub scouts, but they don't have to hit a little ball into 18 holes scattered over three and a half miles.

If the specific goal is long-term, like the thirteen-year-old who says he wants to be No 1, you will need intermediary goals to help along the way. They, too, must be challenging. And they must be goals that can be seen to have been realized as soon as they are achieved. The goal-setting process will become counter-productive and damage your game if you cannot see results along the way. If you planted a lawn and the grass took more than a year to peep through you would have abandoned your goal and covered the whole area in crazy paving before six months were out.

Once you achieve an intermediate goal you boost your confidence with the knowledge that you have accomplished something and proved to yourself that you can do it. When you set target dates for your goals you prevent yourself becoming bored. If you aim to lose twenty pounds in weight before Christmas you will soon become bored unless, in the meantime, you set targets of so much a week or a month; then, if you succeed at the end of a period you grow more confident, and if you miss one of your short-term goals you have a motive for doing better.

The player who says his goal for the day is not to play a bad shot is heading for trouble – he has anything upward of seventy chances of missing his goal. Much better to say he's going to go for seventy good shots. That way one bad shot will not ruin the whole day. The only way to build and bolster confidence is with success. But when you are a beginner, or struggling to begin to improve (as are all golfers) how can you be successful? You are bound to lose. The only way you can have success is to set yourself goals which you can achieve even when you are losing, but goals for which you have to strive.

Thinking about achieving your goals not only contributes to your confidence, also it provides positive expectations about your future performance. If you have set a goal to land fifteen practice chips out of twenty within a putter-length of the hole and you achieve this regularly, you will have only a positive expectation every time you are confronted with a chip shot in future. So the next time your 5-iron approach misses the green, you will still be confident of par.

You will achieve nothing in life or on the golf course unless you have confidence. You do not always have to hang it out for a public airing (the aspect of the American psyche which the British dislike so much); nor do you have to bottle it all up and let out only the self-deprecatory bits (which the Americans think is so very, very British).

Confidence may vaunt itself: 'I can't pat myself on the back enough for the patience and maturity I showed out there today . . . I'm older and wiser, kind of like a wine: I get better with age. I don't have any doubts about myself,' said Payne Stewart, after the third round of the 1993 US Open when he was one stroke behind Lee Janzen, who went on to beat Stewart by the same margin.

Or confidence can complain: '. . . I'm fed up'; '. . . a waste of time'; '. . . just a slog' (Colin Montgomerie, Ian Woosnam and Nick Faldo, after their third rounds in the same championship which they finished respectively 12, 14 and 17 strokes behind the winner).

What good lessons the pros give us when their advice is not being 'ghosted'. You don't have to search for your golfing glory in gaudy knickerbockers, but you can (and should) get better with age, particularly if you don't have any doubts about yourself. On the other hand, if your golf becomes a slog and you feel fed up and it all becomes a waste of time – you should walk away and leave it till next week. Until you've had time to put your goals into some kind of proper perspective.

EIGHT

====

PRESSURE POINTS

Anxiety is the rust of life, destroying its brightness and weakening its power

Tryon Edwards

WHEN DONALD DEGREVE died in 1991 of a heart attack on the 16th green at Winter Haven in Florida his body lay there for two hours as other golfers played through. Thoughtful club officials did cover the body with a sheet. Later one of his three playing partners, Robert Alexander, told *USA Today*: 'It was a real shock to all of us, but there really was nothing we could do. We all thought "Gee, that's a good way to go."' Death on the course is an occurrence that has been visited upon many, probably most, golf clubs at some time. It is not considered a natural hazard of the game because devoted golfers will generally echo the immortal benediction of Donald DeGreve's partner.

We offer no proof, only a suggestion that the incidence of heart attacks and associated afflictions striking (often fatally) on the golf course is a subject worthy of some serious study.

We have all been close to it. At the end of 1993 Greg Norman was playing in the Sydney Classic that bears his name when his pro-am partner, Harry Watts, dropped dead at his feet. Norman summoned an ambulance from his mobile phone (something not all club golfers carry in their golf bags) but the paramedics could do nothing for Watts. Of course, Harry Watts and Donald DeGreve might have died at home or at the office if they had not been out playing golf at a particular moment. Or they might not.

We are quite prepared to believe that walking four miles around a golf course, carrying a bag or pulling a trolley, may be too strenuous a physical activity for some people as they grow older. But the fatalities include just as many golfers who have covered the course in electrically-powered golf carts. Nor can we blame the swing; most golfers as they grow older hit the ball quite effectively with adapted swings that demand little more energy than they employ to slip into their pyjama jackets.

It is more likely that the pressures of the player's life – physical, medical, or mental, or some combination of the three – have been compounded by the game's own stresses. Many golfers see the golf course as a haven where they can escape the pressures of everyday life. They see their round of golf as a way of leaving their cares behind them. What they fail to realize is that if they cannot rid themselves of the pressures of their normal lives while off the course, there is no way their worries, frustrations, and anxieties will take any notice of the Members Only barrier.

But be comforted: golf is not a killer. Any more than motor cars or gas cookers are killers. Misused, most things can be lethal. Played properly, golf can only be good for you.

Golf does possess an excess of ingredients that, in any other context, would be seen as potentially dangerous when added to other life-threatening factors. But if you do not take all your other worries onto the golf course, you may reasonably feel assured that your game will not kill you. Any doctor will tell you that if you allow your worries to accumulate you will have the makings of a heart condition. We say that if you bring those stresses onto the golf course the least that will happen is that your game will suffer. The rest you can work out for yourself.

Stress on the golf course – like anywhere else – comes in a variety of guises. You may try to avoid the provocative word 'stress' by calling it 'pressure', 'strain', or 'tension', but these are no more than euphemisms for stress. And stress has no common denominator. What is stressful for one person may not cause stress in another. What is stressful in one situation may not induce stress in another context.

There is clear scientific evidence of the link between the mind and the body. There is equally convincing evidence that, both at work and play, the same (often unrecognized) pressures that energize us and drive us on can also cause us stress.

Stress is not imposed upon people by external events; stress is induced by the way the individual interprets an event. Stress is all in the mind. And because it has an existence only within your mind, you have total control over it. You can do not only something, but *everything* about it.

The Daily Telegraph sports columnist Michael Calvin sought to rationalize the tension of golfers during the 1994 Open thus: 'It colonises the colon, then moves up through his body until it seizes its victim by the throat.' No-one among the TV-watching millions throughout the world whose own throats were seized by the agony of Bernhard Langer's failed six-foot putt at Kiawah Island (which not only failed to retain the Ryder Cup for Europe but gave it to the United States) would accuse Calvin of hyperbole. But what does become exaggerated out of all proportion is the residue of the stress.

With the last stroke of the 1991 Ryder Cup Langer had what his captain, Bernard Gallacher, later called 'the most stressful putt in the history of golf'. Such a sentiment was understandable, but not so pertinent as Langer's own assessment of the six-footer that trickled round the righthand edge of the hole. 'Lots of people believed I would never recover from that,' he recalled later. 'But I knew I could block it out.'

The picture the world saw of Langer, with strained face, taut body, knees spastically half-bent, fingers tightly clenched, a soundless scream seeking to burst from his locked jaw – this picture does not tell the story of how 'the most stressful putt in the history of golf' caused its maker no 'post-traumatic' stress.

For his team the putt was disastrous – Europe had lost the Ryder Cup. For most other golfers that putt would have imposed enormous stress – and because of the stress probably all of them would have missed the putt, just as Langer did. Of course he was under stress when he made that putt – no six-footer is a gimme. Moreover, for most golfers the stress of having to make that final putt to retain the cup for their team (unbearable though it might have been at that moment) would have been nothing to the follow-up stress that would have affected them.

But Bernhard Langer manages stress better than most golfers on tour. He has been consumed by – and emerged triumphant from – three sustained attacks of what he calls the 'twitches' and the rest of us call the 'yips'. He once told a dinner audience of Christians in Sport: 'If only the world would ask how I've endured such problems and yet remained so content.'

Langer's ability to handle stress – or to put it more accurately, his ability not to allow events on the golf course (and no doubt also in his private life) to be churned by his mind into stress – may well be a by-product of religious beliefs that were reborn in him in 1985 when Larry Mize introduced him to the US Tour's Bible Study Group. But it was not so much religious faith as faith in himself that saved Langer from the stress (and perhaps the lethal after-effects) of that six-footer on Kiawah Island. There was not a viewer among the many millions in every part of the world who did not feel for Langer as his putt detoured around the cup. There was no-one who did not imagine that they could empathize with him. But few will have guessed what he was really thinking. 'The first thing that crossed my mind when I missed the putt was that it was a good thing it happened to me,' he admitted long after the event.

Langer's experience tells us – whether we like to admit it to ourselves or not – that events on the golf course can put pressure on every player. Most of us cannot convince ourselves that we do not and will not let it get to us, because it has done so before and it will again. In fact, anyone who steps out onto a golf course will experience events that *can* cause stress; but not everyone experiences the stress. Very few people know what causes stress, fewer know the effect it has on them, and fewest of all have any idea what they might do about it.

Psychologists sometimes use what they call Life Events Scales to measure how much stress a person may be suffering. A Life Events Scale is made up of things (usually they are events) which occur throughout all our lives and which are generally considered to be in varying degrees stressful. Those events that cause the most stress score high, the least stressful score lowest. In a sample scale, the death of a spouse might rate top marks (100) and Christmas might foot the table at (say) 12. In between could come divorce (73), injury or illness (53), marriage (50), retirement (45), a change in one's financial situation (38), a child leaving home (29), a move to new house (20), a change in sleep pattern (16), or a holiday (13).

If you really are serious about wanting to play your best golf – and why else would you have read this far? –

you must be seriously concerned with reducing your level of stress on the course. We could suggest a general Golf Events Scale, perhaps with maximum stress points (100) for an air shot and a short putt that ends six inches short of the hole at the bottom of the table for 12. In between we could have: out of bounds (73), lost ball (53), left golf shoes at home (50), general rough (45), tendency to slice or hook (38), steep-faced bunker (29), easy approach short of green (20), chip in first cut at edge of green (16), hip flask empty (13).

You might care to draw up your own Golf Events Scale. If you can think dispassionately about your game you will be able to list (in order) those things that give you problems. Allocate points in relation to the effect you think they have on your temperament. When you finish a round (better to wait until you get home) you can tot up your score and see how stressed you were (or still are!).

You should remember, though, that one man's stress rating is not the same as another's. And you have to rationalize the manner in which your overall score is totalled. If you take our Life Events Scale, you will see that a man who goes on holiday five times scores higher (65) than someone who has had an injury or been ill (53). If you land short of the green on three holes you will have a higher stress score (according to our hypothetical table) than if you lose a ball. But you might chip close on all three greens and still make par.

The important thing to keep in mind is that different people interpret different events in different ways. It is not the event that is stressful, it is how you react within yourself to the event. So you may score highly on your scale although you have not felt particularly stressed, just as you might feel you were under terrible pressure and still score very low.

The golfer with a scratch handicap who hooks his drive out of bounds might become unbearable to play alongside for the rest of the round. The newcomer to the game who puts his drive out of bounds 200 yards down the fairway might remember that shot as the best he's ever struck.

Stress has the same beginnings for humans as for animals. Professor Robert Sapolsky of Stanford University in California carried out a fourteen-year study of wild baboons in the Serengeti in East Africa. When they were faced with danger the baboons released stress hormones that shut off their bodies' maintenance and repair systems in order to gather their resources. Stress begins the same way on the golf course as it begins at home or at work, or on the plains of Kenya. Always it is inspired by a threat, or something that we perceive to be a threat, to ourselves. When we recognize this threat it triggers a physiological mechanism known as the 'Fight, Flight or Freeze Response'. This response is automatic and it is vital for our survival. It releases large quantities of hormones into the bloodstream which prime the body for emergency action, the same hormones that evolved millions of years ago in order to prepare our ancestors to fight or to flee.

The main hormones that are released are adrenaline and 17-OHCS, which is better known as cortisol. When a threat is perceived the pituitary gland (at the base of the brain) sends a message by way of various hormones to the adrenal gland (situated above the kidneys). The adrenal medulla then produces adrenaline and shortly afterwards the adrenal cortex begins secreting cortisol. Adrenaline is the chemical responsible for the very rapid preparedness for fight, flight or freeze. It gives every creature the strength to fight or run. Adrenaline accelerates the pulse rate, elevates blood pressure and the rate of the blood circulation in the muscles and stimulates the central nervous system. Adrenaline is the biggest medal winner in track and field.

Cortisol acts to inhibit the inflammation of damaged

tissues – this inflammation often can be more damaging than the actual injury. Cortisol holds down the immune system by regulating the blood-cell types in circulation, particularly by reducing the number of active white blood cells. The immune system is responsible for fighting illness and infection in the body. But this requires a large amount of energy – energy which the organism cannot afford to be without if it has to fight, fly or freeze. In order to survive the body must be able to draw upon all its resources at times of emergency so cortisol is released into the system to depress or switch off the immune system until the fight, flight or freeze mechanism is no longer necessary. Cortisol wins most of its medals in contact and endurance events.

This range of responses: to get stuck in, run like hell, or become rooted to the ground, is universal. Stone-Age man displayed it when he left his cave to catch a mammoth for dinner and stumbled across a sabre-tooth tiger instead. He could fight (but he'd left his spear at home), he could flee (but he knew the tiger was faster) or he could freeze (and hope the tiger wouldn't see him). The rabbit has the same options when it is caught in your car headlights: fighting is an impossible option, fleeing down the road is out because the car is faster, freezing is all that is left.

People freeze for other reasons. Often they panic because of the emotions that clog their mind when they feel threatened. When a cat is lying fast asleep, dreaming whatever it is that cats dream, and a picture falls off the wall with a loud crash, it will awaken with its hackles rising and legs stiff, poised to take one of the three options. When it sees the broken picture on the floor it goes straight back to sleep.

When a human is awakened by the same falling picture the same mechanism is activated but, no matter how hard he tries, he cannot get back to sleep. The mechanism that was set in motion by the sound of the breaking picture continues, though at a lesser intensity. Faster than they can be metabolised, the chemicals flow into the human bloodstream.

The human being *allows* the perceived threat to remain in his head because he continues to rehearse it, to go over it again and again in his mind. He not only recognizes that the picture has fallen off the wall, but also asks why it fell? Was it hung badly? Has it damaged the wall-covering? Is the broken glass causing a danger? Was the picture insured? For how much? What will the insurers say?

Even the next day, the incident will not be forgotten. Every time he enters the room the human being will recall in his mind that falling picture and the emotions it stirred. So his fight, flight, or freeze response will be activated again; it will be less intense, no doubt, but nonetheless those chemicals will be released again (and quite unnecessarily) into the bloodstream.

Such unwarranted replaying of an event is commonplace and can involve what people fear will happen as well as what did happen. Perhaps you had an experience that you found difficult to shake off the last time you played – you may have put three balls in the water on one hole. Next time out, on another course where there is no water, another partner, who is totally unaware of your triple-splash, starts telling you how his daughter has started swimming lessons. The mention of swimming reminds you of water and sets off the emotions again. Along with the emotions, the chemicals start to flow again. And after a while, because they are constantly being released into the system, they will begin to damage the body.

The damage they will do is like the effect lemon juice has on a copper coin. If a coin is left overnight in lemon juice you are right to expect a good result – the coin will emerge clean and bright. This is the same effect fight, flight or freeze chemicals have when they are in the body for a short time – the body becomes primed for action. But if the coin is left in the lemon juice for several days it will corrode and eventually the damage will be permanent. Similarly, if the chemicals are allowed to course too long through the bloodstream they will eventually damage the body. In the short term this damage will manifest itself in irritability and indecision and a lack of both concentration and humour – personality traits that are not unfamiliar on the golf course. Growing stress induces aches and pains, depression and anxiety, irritable bowel syndrome and insomnia. Chronic stress may be a risk factor in heart disease and can raise the risk of cancer.

If cortisol remains in the bloodstream the immune system will continue to be suppressed, which obviously makes the body more vulnerable to illness. If you are one of those people who always seem to be picking up bugs or getting one cold after another, this might well be caused by over-production of cortisol suppressing the immune system. Foreign cells have been allowed to live and multiply without interference. A striking effect of this is the sudden illness often suffered by people recently relieved of prolonged stress. Students normally exhibit considerable powers of endurance in the weeks leading up to an important exam. Then, the day after the examination, they may come down with a very heavy cold. Professor Cary Cooper, of the Manchester Institute of Science and Technology, asks: 'How many people do you know who have done a really big job and then they've taken the next week off work with flu? It's a classic.'

There are other, more serious examples. Sunnie Mann was such a one. For two and a half long years Mrs Mann campaigned tirelessly for the release of her husband Jackie who was being held hostage by terrorists of the Revolutionary Justice Organization who had kidnapped him in Beirut in May 1989. In response to the long-term threat imposed by her husband's captivity, both adrenaline and cortisol were continuously being produced in Sunnie Mann's body. While the cortisol was suppressing her immune system and making her more vulnerable to illness, the adrenaline gave her the strength to carry on. When Jackie Mann was released in September 1991, Sunnie Mann's threat disappeared. The excessive quantities of adrenaline and cortisol that had flowed for so long through her bloodstream returned to normal. But her immune system, rather like a cranky old engine, took a while to get going again. With the vastly-reduced amount of adrenaline in her body to keep her going and with her immune system malfunctioning, Sunnie Mann died of cancer the next year.

Going over and over in your mind whatever it is that has upset you at work or at play is very disabling. At best it will result in depression, anxiety, confusion. At its worst it will cause paranoia, a fear that you are cracking up, a feeling that you are mentally ill and losing touch with reality. This is an extremely unpleasant and upsetting experience, because each time you think about what has upset you, you are setting off on the emotional roller coaster once again. You begin looking inwards on yourself and your attention is not free to concentrate on getting on with the job or the game. If you are not very careful your whole life, when you are meant to be earning a livelihood and when you are trying to make par, will become a waking nightmare. A lot of golfers like to think their gentle activity is quite distinct from the pressures of everyday life that can produce chronic stress disorders. And they are right, unless they are hyper-sensitive or bring on to the course with them a headful of problems from home or work.

If you require proof of how you respond to stress you could take yourself out onto the practice ground and build some self-induced stress. For the sake of the exercise ignore everything you have learned about not aiming and not looking for instant feedback of results. The result we want this time is stress. Set yourself a target and resolve to reach it 20 times. When you have made it 12, 13 and 14 times the tension will begin to mount as every succeeding shot brings you nearer to your goal. If one fails you will have to start the whole thing over again. This may not be a comfortable way of creating pressure, but it is effective.

Colin Montgomerie used to do something like this when he was on a golf scholarship at Houston Baptist University. He would go out on the practice green and set himself the target of making 100 consecutive two-foot putts. When he missed one, he started the whole thing over again. Now that he has become one of the best putters in the world (he thinks – as we would urge him to believe – that he *is* the best in the world) often he tells himself as he stands over a vital putt: 'You've holed these thousands of times before . . .' He tends to strike the ball on 'thousands'.

While shorter practice sessions are the most effective because you learn better when you are fresh (three half-hour sessions are always better than one stint of an hour-and-a-half), this time we want you to get tired and miss your target. This way you will lose confidence and become stressed. And although you probably set out wondering what it was going to be like to suffer golf stress, you will almost certainly find that you feel exactly the same as you feel all too often when playing any round of golf. All those rounds when you told everybody that you never feel any stress and that you cannot understand other people who are always talking about the pressures of the game!

Handling stress on the golf course is something you have to face if you want to play your best golf. Unless, of course, you have mastered the art of playing with an empty mind. Play with an empty mind and you cannot suffer stress because stress, as we have told you, is mind-made. Even if you just cannot get that far and can manage only a Thought for the Day and a good pre-shot routine, at least you will suffer less stress.

No-one else is going to handle your stress for you. Stress counsellors are all very well for convincing you you are going to have a nice day, but when an upsetting event occurs out there on the golf course it is what you say to yourself that either blocks it out or allows it to fester in your mind and cause you stress.

At one time Ian Woosnam started taking orange and multi-vitamin tablets '. . . hoping they'll make me feel better mentally'. They did not seem to have the required effect on his game. Henry Cotton was the only British professional golfer knighted by a monarchy which has traditionally honoured more theatricals than sportsmen. He died (aged 80) in December 1987 knowing of his award 'for services to golf', only a few days before the New Year Honours List was made public. Sir Henry had a uniquely uncomfortable way of handling stress. He got rid of it in his third Open win in 1948 by being sick before every round.

No golfer has been a greater ambassador for the game – and for his country when it most needed one – than Gary Player. He was the only South African sportsman to bestride the world during the forty years in which the world imposed sporting sanctions on his country. In that time he won more than 150 tournaments and nine majors (the Open in 1959, 1968 and 1974, the Masters in 1961, 1974 and 1978, the US Open in 1965 and the US PGA in 1962 and 1972). And he did all this while being openly contemptuous of all those who complain about the pressures of playing golf.

'Athletes are making millions without having to win events and they talk about the pressure!' he says, scornfully. While he was accusing many of his fellow sportsmen of being 'soft and spoiled rotten', he was still

– in his late fifties – spending an hour every day doing 300 sit-ups, squats and stretches and lecturing medical students on self-motivation; always including his own aphorism, 'Luck is the residue of design.'

Like Nick Faldo (and Hogan and Nicklaus before him), Player has regulated his life and his play as assiduously as a marketing strategist or a military tactician. He has found it easier than some of the others to reconcile himself to the reality that the winner is not always the best player, consoling himself (and others) with the adage that complete happiness would be hell on earth.

Because of his total (but not obsessive) self-control, and because he can temper scorn with real concern, Gary Player is a supreme example of how to cope with stress. When he derides his fellow golf professionals who complain of the pressures on them, he is mocking them for crying their anguish all the way to the bank. His definition of luck as 'the residue of design' is a more attractive metaphor than bland talk of making our own luck.

We do not argue with Player – or a handful of the more enlightened of the game's commentators who take the pleas that stress has become too much with a large pinch of salt. But they are wrong if they believe that stress is not an integral part of the golf game, or indeed that it is not an ever-present part of living. In Britain the Department of Health estimates that nineteen million working days (or 50,000 years) are lost every year because of stress-related illnesses, costing the nation almost £4 billion.

It may appear simplistic to say that we cause most of the stress from which we suffer because (at best) we control our emotions and our thoughts very poorly, or (at worst) we are not able to control them at all. Unfortunately, that is the simple truth. In golf, as we have tried to show, it is not our swing that cripples us on the course. It is our thoughts and emotions.

A great many professionals who believe they are too macho to suffer stress, let alone have the need of someone to whom they can confide their emotions, are the same golfers who go to endless trouble and expense to employ the right caddie and then hold on to him for dear life. These caddies are the best of all stress counsellors because they are in the right place at the right time. A session off the course with a professional counsellor before the pro starts his first round might help handle any stress he has brought with him from outside, another session after the round might help him sleep better. But it is the confidant-cum-caddie who is the best counsellor – the one who can give his player confidence when it is most needed, when he is playing his golf.

In his *Thirty Years of Championship Golf*, which he wrote with Herbert Warren Wind, Gene Sarazen recalled taking his farewell of the ageing Skip Daniels who had caddied for him in his 1932 Open win at Sandwich.

> I waved to him as he pedalled happily down the drive, the coat I had given him flapping happily in the breeze, and there was a good-sized lump in my throat as I thought how the old fellow had never flagged for a moment during the arduous grind of the tournament and how he had made good his vow to win a championship for me before he died.

Not many golfers have the luxury of a caddie to carry their bags, let alone bear their emotional baggage. In ground-breaking research in the Work Skills Centre at York University, Dr Derek Roger has come to the conclusion that most of us have to rely on two highly adaptive ways of coping with such emotional baggage. They are known as 'Rational Coping' and 'Detachment' – a couple of related ideas that will deliver every bit as much as they promise. Yet these coping strategies are consistently, though perilously, ignored in modern life. Quite simply, detachment is the strategy of cutting

135

yourself off from the emotions that surround an event. If you are able to detach yourself, then you will be able to cope rationally with the situation. Unhappily, it is not normal for people to be able to do this – on or off the golf course. It is not rational to expect yourself to play to scratch after a long winter lay-off when you have never made even single figures before – and yet we all do it. Usually, the failure that results leads you to become embroiled in the emotions, going over and over upsetting incidents in your mind.

It is all very well for us to tell you not to dwell on negative thoughts, or that you must not waste time thinking about the past or worrying about the future, or that all your thinking should be in the present. The trouble is that the human mind is rather like a muscle, and in the same way that the weightlifter can build up his muscles through training (which is nothing more than regular use), so your mind develops by constant exercise. Unfortunately, because of the kind of use you make of it, your mind is likely to become a large and powerful tool for rehearsing unwanted thoughts. It slides back into the past and forward into the future with the same ease with which the weightlifter's large and powerful muscles get used to handling his weights.

The solution is to train your mind not to rehearse. In some cases you can learn to do this very quickly. In others it may take a little longer. It all depends on how powerful your bad habit of thought-rehearsal has become. Dr Roger has developed the 'Stop – Relax – Listen' system, a unique way of breaking the rehearsal habit and so increasing your chances of performing in a rational and detached manner on the golf course.

Stop – Relax – Listen is the green code of the fairway. It is so simple. The only difficulty is convincing golfers that it works – and then getting them to accept that it will only work for them if they keep at it.

Stop requires little explanation: it means Stop! Stop whatever you are doing, break the cycle of rehearsing things over and over in your mind and come back to the present. Some athletes prevent themselves rehearsing negative thoughts when they are performing by mentally shouting 'Stop!' at themselves. For a split-second they will forget what they were thinking about and in the mental vacuum they have created the negative thought is replaced by a positive thought. The golfer, who is not engaged in a violent or energetic sport, is easily able to go on from Stop to Relax.

Relax is as easy to explain as Stop: it means what it says: Relax! Because the mind and the body are inescapably linked, if the mind is tense then the body will be tense. It is easy for most people to understand this. What many may not realize is that the reverse is just as true: if the body is tense the mind also will be tense. So it follows that the body must be relaxed, and every golfer knows he must relax if he expects to make a good swing. So if we are relaxing our bodies for the sake of our swing, we are also making it easier to deal with any pressure that may be building inside us.

Relaxation can be achieved quite simply. You do not need to go through a progressive programme in order to relax either your mind or your body. All that is necessary is that you become aware of any tenseness in your body and then consciously relax that physical tension (which will also help relieve any tension in the mind).

There are two places in the golfer's body where tension and stress are most obvious and where they most often appear. These are the neck and shoulders and the pit of the stomach. If you give some thought now to these two areas of your body then it is quite likely that you will become aware of some (we hope only slight) unease in one or both places. Having encouraged you to be aware of the tension there, it is only right that we should show you a quick and effective way to get rid of it.

Take a deep breath. Now, as you release it, do two things: first allow your neck and shoulders to slump and go loose as the breath slowly escapes and, at the same time, imagine that you are in an elevator that has suddenly begun to go down. When the doors close and the lift starts to drop, you usually experience a sinking feeling in the pit of your stomach. This is the kind of feeling you need to have as you breathe out. While you are doing these two things try to encourage a relaxed and comfortable feeling to flow through your entire body.

The beauty of this technique is that it can be done anywhere at any time, and without those around you knowing what you are doing. If you are always tense on the tee, let it become a part of your pre-shot routine. It can be as you walk to the tee or as you take your stance. It can be done in the locker room as you are tying your shoelaces, or in the pro shop, or at the starter's window as you collect a scorecard. Losing that sensation of physical tension is just a breath away.

Now that you are stopping and relaxing you have to listen. *Listen* is as straightforward a stage as the first two. It is an ideal way of breaking the habit of constantly going back into the past or forward into the future. If you are listening then you must be in the present.

Even on the golf course there are often many noises which may be stressful. Not just the clicking cameras and noisy spectators which irritate the professionals, but everyday sounds such as dogs barking, aeroplanes or helicopters flying over, traffic noises, or ships' sirens sounding across the links. Some may not find such sounds stressful, but for others they are triggers for stress and may also have stressful associations as a result of past experience. Any of the noises, and many others, can stir up emotional associations in the mind – you may have a dog, you must have a car, you will have been in an aeroplane, you might be nervous of sailing or prone to seasickness. So it is important that, whatever sounds you hear out on the golf course, you do not allow them to distract you from the present. Do not try to shut the sound out; listen to it and accept it for what it is, but do not allow it to trigger a train of thought that takes you away from the present.

If you do find that your mind has begun to wander then you must start all over again: Stop – Relax – Listen. You may find you can manage only a few seconds of listening before your mind wanders again; but the more often you practise Stop – Relax – Listen, the more quickly you will break for good that oppressive habit of rehearsing every little thing that troubles you. And the more your mind will stay in the present – which is where your golf ball lies.

When you are out on the course and everything is peaceful, enjoy the present. Listen to the silence around you and focus on your other senses, too. Look at the beauty of the course, taste the freshness of the heather, enjoy the sensuous feel of the breeze . . . and always remember to smell the roses.

NINE

═══

WHERE THERE'S HOPE

No wise man ever wanted to be younger

Jonathan Swift

A SPORTING PHENOMENON occurred in Las Vegas on 6 November 1994 when a sometime world champion and latter-day Texas preacher called George Foreman traded four 'hamhocks and chitlins' for the 369 punches he had taken on his own 250-pound body in the previous nine rounds.

An editorial in *The Times* waxed lyrical:

> It seemed that all America joined in the euphoria of the 45-year-old grandfather who defied age, flab and the derisive predictions of boxing experts to win a tenth-round knock-out victory over a man nineteen years his junior. The young at heart everywhere should join them.

Continuing in the same punch-drunk vein, *The Times* leader proclaimed that Foreman had 'redeemed his own and the sport's reputation'. The risen-again pugilist proclaimed:

> The demographics will never disappear now. On this planet we will always know that the athlete of all athletes is between 45 and 55. So all of you out there thinking, 'I don't know if I can do it any more', remember: If I can do it, you can do it.

140

So it took sport's most hyped discipline to fortify the over-forties with proof that those who would have us believe that there is no future after forty, that fifty is post-middle age, that we are senile by our sixties and impotent by our seventies, are wrong.

Youth (which embraces all until they reach the Big Four-Oh!) is supposed to be everything. Only the young, we are taught, have the strength in body and mind to exploit their talent. Now this is, and always has been, abject nonsense. In most sport – and most certainly in golf at any level – talent does not count the years. But though it required a farce in the boxing ring to prove that there is always hope for all of us, Mr Foreman's $65-million-worth of hamhocks and chitlins will be a feast we can enjoy into our dotage.

There is always hope in golf, as much for the sixty- and seventy-year-old as for the teenager. If you have not got down to scratch (or perhaps even single figures) by the time you are in your fifties, it does not mean that you never will. All the things we have discussed so far have borne out our faith that anyone who follows our advice can become a better golfer. Many of our suggestions will do more for you than that: they will allow you to continue improving your game for many, many years. We are not solely concerned to make you a better player now; we want to encourage you, and show you how to become an even better player in the year 2000 or whenever.

Top athletes in so many sports complain that age is an impediment, and in some sports this is undoubtedly true. But even in physically demanding events it is not the barrier many competitors and commentators would have us believe. An older athlete who beats a younger favourite is not a freak of nature; the fact is that older competitors always have done well. Today, unfortunately, they too often seem to lose the will to continue their winning ways.

Often it is not his strength or skill that deserts the world famous athlete, but his motivation. Nothing throws the inner drive out of gear more than having to live out of a suitcase and sleep in business class while the profits lie in wait at the bank. The money-conscious *mores* of the day have rewarded the sportsman well and taught him to play to live rather than to live to play. So he has as many commercial goals as he has playing goals. And if the commercial goals have already been realized while some of his sporting goals remain to be conquered, the player's motivation inevitably suffers.

It is not just difficult, it is impossible to imagine that any of today's pros will still be winning tour events when they are 52 years and 10 months old, as Sam Snead was when he won the Greater Greensboro Open in 1965. Fourteen years later, when he was 67, he became the only US PGA Tour player ever to beat his age when he had a round of 66 in the Quad Cities Open in Bettendorf, Iowa. Nor is any Open winner likely to return to mark the fiftieth anniversary of his first championship – and not only play the first eight holes under par, but score a hole-in-one – as Gene Sarazen did in 1973 on the Postage Stamp eighth at Royal Troon when he was 71. Playing honorary rounds with former Open winners Max Faulkner and Fred Daly, Sarazen hit his 5-iron into a gentle breeze on the shortest of all Open Championship holes (126 yards). It pitched short of the flag and rolled in. At the same hole the next day his tee shot went in the bunker far below the green on the right – and he holed out with his sand wedge for a birdie.

While young golfers may marvel at the endurance of a man like Sarazen, they should also remember him for what he did for them. It was Sarazen who experimented with lead solder on the back of his niblicks to produce a club that would rebound when it hit the sand, instead of digging in. That is how the sand wedge comes to be in all our golf bags today.

It is believed that the human body achieves its optimum condition in our early twenties. But golf requires neither great strength nor perfect physique. Even if our chosen sport did require muscle we should not be much worse off twenty years after we had peaked, because by the time we reach forty we should have lost no more than ten per cent of our physical power – which may be a factor in some sports, but not in all.

Golf is one of the least physical sports. More than most others, though, it relies heavily on the development of skill. And because the skills of golf are many and varied, there is more scope for improvement than in less complex, single-skill sports. While others must worry about speed or strength, our sole concern is skill. This is not to be confused with talent, which is a God-given genetic superiority. Golf skill is an ability that is produced entirely by practice. And every golfer, of whatever ability, has the potential to improve over many years by proper practice.

In 1956 Dr E.R.F.W. Crossman described a study he had carried out at the Imperial Tobacco Company on women who were employed on piece-rates to make cigars. The cigars were made by machines in two stages, called 'bunch-making' and 'wrapper-laying'. In the bunch-making process women (aged between fifteen and fifty) had to lay binder leaf on a miniature flatbed. The machine ejected a quantity of filler leaf and rolled the binder round this, making a cylinder. The operator then transferred the cigar to a drum in the other half of the machine which put on the wrapper. The bunch-making operation took about four seconds for each cigar. It is difficult to imagine any factory operation that could be more intrinsically boring.

Yet when Crossman studied these women he found that, despite having rolled ten million cigars over seven years, they were still getting better at it. Their skill had become so great that the machines were no longer able to keep up with them. Even the most patriotic Cuban would find it difficult to imagine that the women found pleasure in rolling these cigars. They did not have to, because they had goals instead. And the goals were achievable and ever-present. The more cigars they rolled (and they were all checked for quality) the more money they were paid. So their skill in this most mundane and fleeting operation was continuing to improve even after carrying out the same actions ten million times during the seven-year study – because they were motivated. And because human beings have such a vast capacity for expertise.

If we translate these findings onto the golf course we should have to hit 500 practice balls five days a week for 76 years (which is more than an average lifetime) in order to achieve a total of ten million. And, more-over, such skill (and it was minimal) as was involved in laying down a cigar leaf for it to accept a filling of tobacco and then transferring the cigar tube to a drum to be wrapped, it was one single skill. Hitting a golf ball requires several skills, and hitting 500 balls nearly every day for 76 years is an impossible imposition. But if cigar-rollers can still improve their skill after seven years of practice, how much more can the golfer improve his more pleasant and enjoyable skills over a lifetime.

In fact, your golf skill will never stop improving – unless you want it to. Another of the sins of omission visited upon young golfers by their tutors is the failure to teach them that there is scope (which rhymes with hope) for their skill to go on improving for ever. Because they do not expect to continue to improve for as long as they play the game, many young golfers feel that if they have not made it (whatever 'it' happens to be) by the time they have reached their early twenties, then there's no hope: they think they will never get any better. They could not be more wrong, either about themselves or their game.

There is always scope for considerable improvement – no matter how good you may be. If you set the right goals for yourself, if you continue to practise in the proper way, you can only get better and better. Gary Player says golf is the one game that, if you look after your diet, your fitness, and your mind, you can play well into your seventies. 'What's more,' he says, 'someone on a 20-handicap can beat the best in the world!'

Julius Boros won the US PGA championship in 1968 when he was 48; 'Old Tom' Morris was 46 when he won his fourth Open in 1867 and Jack Nicklaus was the same age when he won the Masters in 1986; Hale Irwin was 45 when he won the US Open at Medinah in 1990, and Harry Vardon and Roberto de Vicenzo both were 44 when they won the Open in 1914 and 1967 respectively. Vardon's was the last of his six Open wins, which is still a record. Six years later, when he was 50, he was runner-up to Edward Ray in the US Open. The oldest winner of the British amateur championship was the Hon. Michael Scott who was 54 when he won the title at Hoylake in 1933, and Jack Westland was 47 when he won the United States amateur championship at Seattle in 1952.

A retired cleric called Harold Snider was 75 when he had three holes-in-one on the Ironwood par-3 course in Phoenix, Arizona, in 1976. F.L. Callender was three years older when he was beaten 4 and 2 in the ninth and final round of the Jubilee Vase at St Andrews in 1932. In 1975, and again ten years later, George Swanwick holed-in-one at his Wallasey club in Cheshire; he was 75 and 85 at the times.

Arthur Thompson was 103 years old when he equalled his age at Uplands Golf Club in British Columbia and George Selbach was going round his Crystal River course on Florida's Gulf coast in 77 when he was 95 years old and sinking two holes-in-one when he was a year older. He had begun playing golf when he was 48 and he never had a lesson. 'I was never one for all that foolishness,' he said. 'I had a theory that you just worked hard on what you knew you could do.' What George Selbach could do was play to scratch into his sixties and still have a 17-handicap when he was 105.

So there is nothing unusual about older golfers playing well. What is extraordinary is the gullibility of those of us who have allowed ourselves to be misled into believing that older is *passé*. Society has become fixated on youth, which only proves that PR hype has more influence than common sense.

The reasons the young are better at many sports is, first of all, because everyone expects them to be better. Secondly, because they are young and enthusiastic and can still dream dreams, the young practise harder and more regularly. Thirdly, because they feel themselves becoming better, it is easier for them to be more motivated than older people. But athletes who confidently expect to continue improving through their forties and fifties (and beyond) are the sportsmen who will outplay their dreams.

The Seniors Tour in the United States produces so much attractive golf and attracts so much spectator interest because none of its players would be taking part if they had not had so many years before their fiftieth birthday in which to develop their skils on that other tour. They would not be out there if they did not have their goals, if they did not have hope. And that is something that cannot be said of all who play the regular tours.

Whenever very young boys play football (or any other team game) there will be the one who stands out from the others. The envious parents of other children may attribute his ability to some genetic fluke, but, unless a youngster happens to be unusually tall and plays basketball, or happens to be particularly short and is keen on gymnastics, you can ignore any hereditary advantage. To suggest that what we call 'talent' must be inherited is merely to admit that we have failed to produce any alternative hypothesis to explain what is simply a slightly superior performance. We do not deny that some athletes – like anyone who performs a skill – may have some ability that is inherent. But we do claim that this is only a basic ability; certainly not some God-given 'talent' that will endow them with greatness. The golfer need not worry about such things, his game is the greatest equalizer in all sport. Indeed, the gods of golf often seem to display a sense of humour: the big, fat man is often the one with the best touch and the little fellow regularly hits the ball farthest.

It is a dangerous misconception to assume that youngsters who display a supposedly innate talent will rapidly scale the heights once they have mastered some basic skills. When today's young geniuses of football are three or four years down the road the 'talent' will probably have disappeared, and even if they are still regularly selected, they no longer stand out: their teammates will have caught up with their precosity.

No-one has ever become a chess grandmaster without at least ten years' intensive practice. There is scientific evidence that the same is true in swimming, tennis, distance running, mathematics and music. Perhaps even more significantly for us, it has been proved that chess players who started to learn the game late in life (after they were eleven years old!) took an average of 11.7 years to reach international chess master level; those who began before they were eleven years old took much longer, 16.5 years, to reach the same level. So the modern teaching pro's theory that to make it big a young golfer needs to take up the game before his age reaches double figures and have a handicap in low single figures before he comes of age, is wildly speculative.

You must never lose hope of improving your performance, whether it is at rolling cigars, playing chess or competing with your regular golfing partner. If you practise your game, if you practise patience, and if you understand, deep down inside yourself, that you do have scope for improvement, you will keep your hope alive. Provided you do these things – and all the other things we have suggested in previous chapters – you will improve more than your partner. Your only problem will come if he takes all our advice, too!

Too often, the diminishing performance of competitors as they grow older is due not to a diminution of the body's potential but to an increase in our faculty for pessimism. We too easily accept, as we grow older, the idea that we are less capable than we really are. And loss of physical prowess should be compensated for by growing wisdom. But this will not happen if we begin to see ourselves as we believe others (younger) see us; if we start to worry more about looking foolish in younger eyes if we hit a bad one; if we think back on the one thing above all others we should not dwell upon: if we reflect upon our lost youth.

In at least one major tournament every year golf produces a riddle as baffling to coaches and commentators, and probably to players as well, as it is to the rest of us. It happened twice in the 1994 United States Open Championship at Oakmont. The leader after the first round was 44-year-old Tom Watson on 68 (3-under par) and second place overnight, one shot behind him, was shared by 54-year-old Jack Nicklaus and a 24-year-old South African called Ernie Els. It would be easy to say that Els went on to win the title that year because, whether or not he could give any strokes to Nicklaus and Watson, he could give them 30 and 20 years respectively. But that is not the reason why the younger man won, nor is it the reason why mature players (a nicer word than 'ageing') so often lead an opening round before they begin to slip down the leaderboard.

It is always risky (not to say invidious) to ascribe motive to anyone, largely because even the most intelligent and objectively self-analytical of human beings are so prone to misinterpret their own motives. It is all too easy to profess a desperate desire to achieve something when really you do not care all that much. You can fool all people, even yourself; but you cannot fool your mind.

Older players who have been there before, who have done everything, won everything, may no longer have the motivation they once had. Their problem is certainly not due to any physiological ageing process. A mental ageing process, perhaps; but even then it is not that they are mentally incapable of winning the big one again. More likely their inner drive has diminished. The need to win has certainly departed long ago, the want is not so urgent and the hope not so desperate. The motivation is not what it was.

There is no doubt that if they can go round a course like Oakmont in a temperature in the high 90s and shoot a 68 and a 69, they can do it another day; even three more days. But there may be doubt – their own doubt – that they can do it again. They may begin to wonder if they really should be topping the leaderboard, asking themselves if they should be doing this at all. Simple, understandable questions to ask oneself in one's mid-forties and fifties. But negative – and hope-less.

We always retain the potential for improving in our work and play. This was first shown around a hundred years ago by Bryan and Harter who discovered that when performers had gone for a long time without improving their skill, they did get better when there was the incentive of a reward. This was proved in 1897 with Morse code operators whose skill had reached a plateau after a lifetime of experience. Given the incentive of promotion and payment for improved performance, their skill suddenly began to get better. This conclusion was confirmed soon after when another research study found that typesetters in a printing works who had been doing the same job for ten years improved their skills over a five-month period by between 58 per cent and 97 per cent – when they were offered bonuses.

Obviously, although the Morse code operators and the typesetters had performed their respective skills at the same consistent level over long periods, something had in fact been happening – they had been accumulating the potential for an improved performance. In the same way, when our golf game seems to be on a plateau, when we can see no obvious improvement, when our handicap remains fixed – all the time when nothing seems to be happening we may, in fact, be improving.

It is fatally easy to give up when our golf skills do not advance at the same rate as our careers off the course. But gaining skill is not like climbing a promotion ladder. Skill levels can be getting higher while apparently standing still. Professional players, particularly, find play on the plateau extremely frustrating. When they do not feel themselves improving, when they cannot see themselves approaching their goals, they become frustrated and begin to panic about their game; and because they neither see improvement nor hope of it, they lose confidence in themselves and their golf.

Plateaus when nothing appears to be happening for long periods will occur often in a lifetime of golf. These are periods when you will be convinced that you are playing well, but you are not scoring any better. So you will begin to doubt that you can be playing well, and you will start to play not so well. This is the danger time when you could lose hope – and then the game, too.

If it is any consolation, the plateaus the pros experience last longer than most of the plateaus of club golfers. Nicklaus stuck on a plateau for three years at the end of the 60s, and all the others have gone through them at least once; some have never moved off them. Unless you know what is happening it is likely that your plateau will become your peak; at best you will stay where you are, at worst you will tumble down the other side.

The plateau in performance has many names. It has been called (pretty accurately) the 'Plateau of Despond'. More clinically it may be categorized as an 'arrested development'. In fact it may be nothing more than a phantom plateau, because although your improvement could have come to a standstill your more important learning processes may be continuing.

An unusual study was carried out in Germany in 1954 in which older athletes were tested against those not-so-old. The tests were not exercises in agility but were explosively athletic. Groups of women aged 32 and 45, both of which had been in regular training, competed against each other in the sprint, shot putt and long jump. The levels of performance achieved by the two groups were inseparable. The two groups of men tested were 40-year-olds who had not trained for the test and 60-year-olds who had trained. The trained 60-year-olds were the faster sprinters. If practice doesn't make you perfect, it will certainly keep you going.

It is extremely rare for any active sportsman to reach a physiological limit. Somewhere out there must be a time or a distance or a height that is beyond any individual's physical ability. But over hundreds of years of striving man has not yet reached these limits. He has not reached the ultimate mile, or throw, or jump because he has continued to be motivated and to hope and to practise. In golf the ultimate limit is certainly way beyond any limit the average player might imagine for himself. So the golfer who reaches a plateau when he cannot feel or see any improvement should never fear being stuck there for ever.

If you can motivate yourself to play through your plateau, you will be learning all the time. Your skill will be undergoing a latent improvement which will lie hidden until it is ready to force its way out into the open. This is when you will experience that dramatic drop in your handicap. Earlier when it was coming down, it would have reduced gradually. Now it will come down several, or perhaps even many, strokes – all at once.

But you must have played and practised through your plateau. A hundred years ago when they were assessing those Morse code operators, Bryan and Harter also studied a group of telegraphy students. In the early days of their training the students improved steadily and they could see and feel themselves getting better. Then they all entered a period of several months when there was no apparent improvement. This was well before they had reached the level of experts, in fact none of them was sufficiently competent to get a job. Some of them became despondent and gave up, others maintained their motivation, practised through their plateaus, and suddenly improved beyond recognition and obtained the hoped-for jobs.

For the club golfer who realizes he will never be a Nicklaus it might be wise not to stay on the plateau for three years. When hope begins to diminish, it is a good time to take the fundamentals to the pro shop for a diagnostic check. The bodywork will be all right and there will be nothing wrong with the engine, but you might need a slight adjustment of the grip, or something just as basic.

When we started out to help you play your best golf more of the time, we never promised to make you a better golfer – only to bring out the best that always has been within you. And you will only achieve your best if your realize that with patience you have the ability to go on improving for ever.

We have shown you how you can consistently get the best results from whatever fundamental skills you have;

how to stop yourself thinking about all those how-to-play instructions that have been cramping your game for years; how to ignore all the distractions in the game; how to stop 'technique' spoiling your performance. We hope you might have come to appreciate the wisdom in the advice Gary Player gave to his young compatriot Ernie Els. 'Stay away from all those coaches,' he urged him. 'There are no better teachers than Trial and Error.'

In golf always there will be hope. Hope is the good companion of the lifetime golfer. George Foreman did not live in peace with himself for the twenty years that followed the rumble in the jungle in Zaire when he was knocked out and humiliated by Muhammad Ali in the eighth round on 30 October 1974. He had won the title in Kingston, Jamaica (beating Joe Frazier), successfully defended it in Tokyo (against Joe Roman) and Caracas (against Ken Norton) and lost it to Ali in Kinshasa. He had never fought a world title fight in the home of the brave until he regained the crown in 1994.

Foreman should not be remembered in the annals of sport as the man who came back after twenty years to become the oldest world heavyweight champion in the history of professional boxing. We should remember him best for reminding us that there is for ever hope.

In golf, much more than in boxing, hope is always justified. As Ogden Nash so eloquently put it . . .

> Oh where this side of the River Styx
> Will you find an equal mate
> To the scorn of a man with a seventy-six
> For a man with a seventy-eight.
> I'll tell you a scorn that mates it fine,
> As the welkin mates the sun:
> The scorn of him with a ninety-nine
> For him with a hundred and one.